Apocalypse Later
Books by Hal C F Astell

Cinematic Hell
Huh? An A-Z of Why Classic American Bad Movies Were Made

Filmography Series
Velvet Glove Cast in Iron: The Films of Tura Satana

Festival Series
The International Horror & Sci-Fi Film Festival 2012

Apocalypse Later
Filmography Series

Velvet Glove Cast in Iron:

The Films of Tura Satana

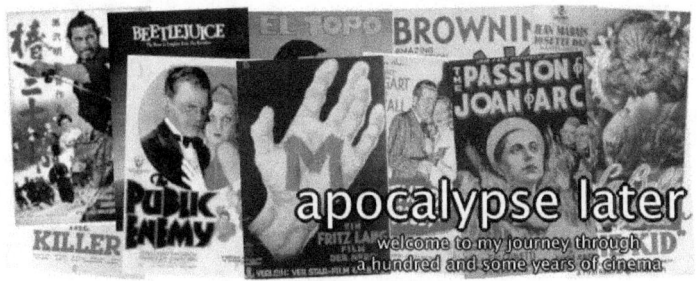

Apocalypse Later Press
Phoenix, AZ

Apocalypse Later Filmography Series
Velvet Glove Cast in Iron: The Films of Tura Satana

ISBN-10: 0989461319
ISBN-13: 978-0-9894613-1-3
Catalogue reference number: ALP002

Reviews by Hal C F Astell

These reviews originally appeared, albeit
in evolutionary form, at Apocalypse Later
http://www.apocalypselaterfilm.com

Front cover art by Keith Decesare
http://www.kadcreations.com

Foreword by Peaches Christ
http://www.peacheschrist.com

Afterword by Cody Jarrett
http://www.tropicofilm.com

Published through CreateSpace
https://www.createspace.com

Typeset in Gentium
http://scripts.sil.org/FontDownloadsGentium

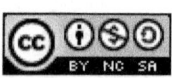

"You're cute, like a velvet glove cast in iron.
And like a gas chamber, Varla, a real fun gal."

- Billie, *Faster, Pussycat! Kill! Kill!*

Dedication

This book was always going to be for Andrea Beesley, known far and wide as the Midnite Movie Mamacita.

Thank you, Andrea, for being the Goddess of Grindhouse in the Phoenix metropolitan area. Your programming at venues across the valley has enabled me to see more outrageous pictures, from the amazing to the abysmal, on the big screen and often in 35mm, than I ever would have dreamed possible, including one reviewed here.

Since we met at the International Horror & Sci-Fi Film Festival in 2007, purely by chance because one of your friends heard me speak and erroneously thought I was a Kiwi like you, the highlights are too numerous to mention.

Even sticking merely to film, it's hard to choose the best of the best, but I'll try. Your allowing me to screen *Freaks* at the Royale was a special treat. Watching the original *The Wizard of Gore* at Farrelli's while eating delicious steak was surreal. Experiencing a Jodorowsky double bill at Chandler Cinemas, which was at the exact same time hosting a rave, a Hindi movie and a film for the deaf, was beyond surreal. The first screening of *The Room* with Denny hiding in plain sight in the audience was magical. Live parkour at MADCAP for the *District B13* sequel was a riot. Seeing Fulci's *Zombie* without sound but with Dutch subtitles is the only way to go. The fifties Corman triple bill was a personal joy for me. The Thanksgiving Feast movie marathon, fuelled by Steven Seagal energy drinks, was priceless.

I'll never forget my first film at the Royale, *Hobo with a Shotgun*, or the many which followed. I still miss that little theatre.

Then there are your years of festival programming and the wide range of guests you've brought to the valley, from Lance Henriksen to Kitten Natividad, via Crispin Glover and Tommy Wiseau.

Surely your only failing is that you brought out some of those guests, like Tura Satana and Ted V Mikels, before I knew who you were or what you were doing. I guess I forgive you.

And if these reminiscences spark enthusiasm in locals who were there or wish they could have been, in 2013 Andrea is presenting her Ms Behaving series at FilmBar in Phoenix, "highlighting wicked women, lethal ladies and bad girls in film." See you there.

Acknowledgements

No book is ever created by one person, regardless of whose name is on the cover. Many other people deserve credit, along with my undying gratitude and appreciation for their part in bringing this one to print. Thank you, one and all!

Most obviously, thanks to Dee Astell, my long suffering better half. She doesn't just get to watch everything I review, good, bad or worse. She also gets to relive those experiences over again as I read my rough draughts to her aloud in a rather masochistic version of proofreading, so that she can politely point out all my mistakes and misunderstandings. Any she missed are my fault entirely.

Thanks to Bob Nelson, multimedia magnate at the burgeoning Brick Cave Publishing empire, who continues to be not only a wealth of knowledge about the technical side of the publishing process but someone who happily puts up with all my questions.

Thanks to Keith Decesare, versatile artist extraordinaire, for fully realising what I envisioned for the cover and then some. If you think his work here is great, check out his amazing steampunk ladies and tell him I sent you.

Thanks to the glamorous and glorious Peaches Christ for her foreword, and to the elegant and eloquent Cody Jarrett, director of *Sugar Boxx*, for his afterword. I'm honoured by your colourful and insightful contributions to my little book.

Special thanks to Tura Satana, for blessing us with ten films and three episodes of TV shows, however briefly she may have appeared in many of them. Her place in cinematic history was ensured after her third feature. Everything else was just a bonus.

Contents

How Much Tura?

Irma la Douce (1963)
As a pretty in purple Parisian prostitute, Tura is on screen a lot, but mostly only to provide exotic background colour. She also has a few lines of dialogue here and there.

Who's Been Sleeping in My Bed? (1963)
Tura is an uncredited stripper in a Tijuana bar, dancing on stage behind the characters focal to the scene.

Burke's Law: Who Killed the Paper Dragon? (1964)
A more conventional dancer this time, Tura provides the motion in an early scene in a Chinese restaurant. She gets one line.

The Man from UNCLE: The Finny Foot Affair (1964)
As the second in command to a Japanese general, the villain of the piece, Tura has a lot of screen time and looks menacing throughout. It doesn't show what she was capable of but it certainly hints at it.

Faster, Pussycat! Kill! Kill! (1965)
This is Tura's best part and only lead rôle. Top billed, she dominates throughout as the film's driving force (pun intended) and the sheer personification of female power. It's the first and last word in the world of Tura on screen.

Our Man Flint (1966)
Uncredited once more, Tura plays another stripper in another bar scene, this time in Marseille. At least it's an important scene.

The Girl from UNCLE: The Moulin Ruse Affair (1967)
As the leader of the villain's all-female Elite Guard, Tura does look awesome but she has far too little to do.

The Astro-Zombies (1968)
As a mysterious, exotic and powerful foreign agent, Tura leads one of the subplots. This is her biggest rôle in a feature outside of *Faster, Pussycat! Kill! Kill!*

The Doll Squad (1973)
We meet eight members of the Doll Squad during this picture. Tura plays one of the six who make it to the main mission, though not the most obvious. She's an exotic dancer by day and an electronics expert by night.

Mark of the Astro-Zombies (2002)
As the sister of her character in *The Astro-Zombies*, Tura leads a new but just as nefarious subplot.

Sugar Boxx (2009)
As a Florida judge who sends the heroine to prison, Tura only gets one scene early on but it comes with a good, if short, monologue.

The Haunted World of El Superbeasto (2009)
Tura briefly reprises Varla, her character from *Faster, Pussycat! Kill! Kill!*, for a cameo in this animated feature.

Astro-Zombies: M3 - Cloned (2010)
Tura appears briefly in holographic form in old footage from *The Astro-Zombies*, but provides new dialogue.

Velvet Glove Cast in Iron: The Films of Tura Satana

Foreword
by Peaches Christ

For those of you unfamiliar with my work, I'm a filmmaker and cult leader working in San Francisco. My *Midnight Mass* movie series was born out of my sincere and deep love of cult cinema and the first ever show I produced back in 1998 was for a screening of *Faster, Pussycat! Kill! Kill!*

I was first introduced to the Russ Meyer classic through John Waters's book *Shock Value* when he said the film is "the best movie ever made, and possibly better than any movie that will ever be made." Through John's seminal book about his own career I was able to discover the work that inspired him.

In no small part, *Faster Pussycat*'s success must be credited to the star of the film, the incomparable Tura Satana: an on-screen spectacle, the likes of which had never been seen before *or since*. She has inspired countless numbers of us with her confident combination of strength and sex. As Peaches Christ, I worshipped and embodied Ms Satana to the best of my abilities.

For that first Pussycat event I hosted a "Tura Satana look-a-like contest" in her honor. Of course no onstage imitation can compare to the real deal so it was truly mind-blowing when I invited the *actual* Tura Satana to come do my *Midnight Mass* show some years later and she accepted the invitation, came to San Francisco and appeared before an audience of rabid, obsessed fans like myself. The event was billed as an evening of "Idol Worship at the altar of Tura Satana".

When she hit the stage the audience exploded, rose to their feet and gave her a standing ovation that would not stop. When she and I finally sat down and had our on stage conversation I was *super* nervous but I soon knew I was sitting next to a true show business pro. I was realizing that in some way Tura actually was Varla: a strong woman completely in control of the situation and able to handle the hundreds of men *and women* she was seducing and intimidating with every word she uttered.

The energy in the theatre was electric and she had us gripped by stories of her career, also talking about behind-the-scenes moments from her own incredible life. Tura shared tales about herself that were more exciting, more heroic, and more adventurous than the life of any of the exciting characters she played on screen. This show was such a success that she and I took it on the road and performed together in Seattle, Los Angeles, San Diego, etc.

When my *Midnight Mass* movie event celebrated its tenth anniversary, I was in the unique position to actually introduce John Waters to Tura Satana for the first time. That was a brunch I will NEVER forget!

Tura and I became close friends over the years and her impact on my life cannot be measured. I'm thrilled to read Hal's new book and filmography of this great star because it's an important document of an incredible woman's unique career. It will inevitably help fans further discover Tura and her work much like I did through John's book. I hope folks that have only seen *Pussycat* are inspired to seek out other classics like *The Doll Squad* and *The Astro-Zombies* and that this book leads them there.

Her filmography is fascinating in part because each film is another marker in the life of one of the most exciting actresses to exist and I hope someday the whole world will know all about the kick-ass life of Tura Satana.

Peaches Christ
2013

Velvet Glove Cast in Iron: The Films of Tura Satana

Velvet Glove Cast in Iron: The Films of Tura Satana

Introduction

I was a long way behind the curve. Tura Satana's groundbreaking performance in *Faster, Pussycat! Kill! Kill!* had stunned and thrilled audiences for a couple of decades before I heard about it in the mid eighties and finally saw it a few years later.

It's difficult to explain just how impossible it was to be a fan of exploitation cinema in England during that decade, even to similar fans in other countries but especially to the generation who have grown up on the internet. To most people, it's simply impossible not to be able to see something. If it's not streaming on NetFlix, it can usually be bought on Amazon. If it isn't commercially available, the PirateBay probably has it for free. It might even be a click away on YouTube. We're getting close to a post-scarcity world.

For me, I had to experience movies like Tura's by proxy: through books, magazines and the occasional TV documentary. I could read about all sorts of fascinating and enticing material in the history books, in magazines like *The Dark Side* or in the slew of zines I was devouring like *Trash City* that hinted at a tape trading circuit that I only dreamed of being a part of.

What I couldn't do was actually watch most of these films. Some were banned and video shop owners were actually going to jail for daring to rent something deemed legally obscene. With the BBFC unlikely to approve many films for release, distributors often didn't bother even paying the fee to hear them say no. I did buy as many videos as I could: new releases, ex-rentals and whatever overpriced bargains I could persuade market stall owners to sell me under the table at car boot sales. I couldn't pick and choose though. I bought whatever was available and that wasn't much.

Occasionally one of the four television channels I had to choose from would show something more outrageous than a lurid Hammer horror, usually BBC2 because art films could be outrageous too; just ask Peter Greenaway or Ken Russell. Best of all was an outstanding late night series of cult films called *Moviedrome*, presented by film director Alex Cox, which introduced me to so much. I owe it a great debt and it's a major reason why my personal tastes in film are as inquiring and eclectic as they are.

Most pertinent here was a fascinating but annoyingly brief series of documentaries presented by Jonathan Ross, enticingly titled *The Incredibly Strange Film Show*. Each week, Ross would explore the career of an underground exploitation legend, showing clips from their films, visiting them in person and interviewing them and anyone else who was available who could add a valid perspective. If *Moviedrome* expanded my horizons, *The Incredibly Strange Film Show* set me to compiling lists of what I needed to track down at any cost.

Season one was a godsend to an exploitation addict who couldn't find many places to get a fix. After exploring the work of John Waters, Ray Dennis Steckler and Herschell Gordon Lewis, Ross focused on Ted V Mikels and then Russ Meyer.

Both are fascinating characters in their own right, worthy of their own filmography books like this, if only I can ever track down those last few elusive titles, but they were prominent directors of Tura Satana, who was featured in both episodes. To put it mildly, I hadn't seen anything like her before. In particular, I'd never seen anything like *Faster, Pussycat! Kill! Kill!* before, and only being able to see mere clips was akin to torture. I just had to track films like that and *The Astro-Zombies* down. It became something of a mission.

By the end of the eighties, I took to reading program listings for satellite channels, even though we didn't have satellite at home. A colleague at work had satellite and she was kind enough to tape movies for me that I could never see anywhere else. So it was that I managed to finally see Varla strut her majestic stuff at last. It was everything I'd hoped and expected it would be and more. I may not have loved it as much as John Waters, whose one sheet for the film was prominently displayed during his interviews for *The Incredibly Strange Film Show*, but then I'm not sure anyone ever has. I loved it nonetheless and, even then, it felt like a milestone.

It took a long time to find the rest of her work. For someone who changed the face of cinema, her screen career was maddeningly short: just ten features and, according to IMDb, only three episodes of TV shows. I hear about others, tantalisingly mentioned in some of her more substantial obituaries, but don't have solid information on them yet. If I can ever track them down, maybe this book will see an expanded edition.

Apparently she obtained her Screen Actors Guild card playing a secretary on a detective show called *Hawaiian Eye*, maybe as early as the late fifties; it ran for four seasons, starting in 1959. I've read that she appeared on the TV adaptation of Cecil B DeMille's circus picture, *The Greatest Show on Earth*, perhaps as a recurring character. One obituary mentions a sitcom called *Valentine's Day*, which played for a season back in 1964. Maybe more research will turn up more appearances, but however many, it still wasn't enough.

As you'll find within this book, as I explore every one of the film and television appearances that she's credited with, she often had a small part in proceedings. Her powerful rôle as Varla isn't merely her most iconic performance, it's also her best and her largest. Clearly Hollywood was scared stiff of her, but indie producers didn't seem to have a clue how to put her to best use either.

She'd come to acting from the stage, where she had found a home in burlesque and on the exotic dancing circuit. All too soon, she had retired from acting too. After she made *The Doll Squad* for Ted V Mikels in 1973, she found her way into nursing instead, not to return to the screen until 2002. Later she would shift career again, becoming a police dispatcher and the wife of a retired cop.

She lived a truly amazing life, one that seems designed for a big screen biopic. She was gang raped at nine, but learned martial arts and, over fifteen years, systematically extracted her revenge. She posed nude for Harold Lloyd, who didn't know she was underage; it was he who suggested a film career to her. She dated Elvis Presley, and allegedly turned him down when he proposed. She danced on Sunset Strip. She was shot by a former lover. She broke her back in a car crash. Cody Jarrett, who directed her in *Sugar Boxx*, is adapting her unpublished memoir and I can't wait.

However, her legacy is always going to begin with Varla, because she changed the lives of people who never met her and the course of American film in the process. *Faster, Pussycat! Kill! Kill!* was not a great success on initial release, but it grew and it continues to grow today. It remains the pinnacle on film, not of female equality but of feminine superiority. And frankly, who's going to top it?

Hal C F Astell
Apocalypse Later
2013

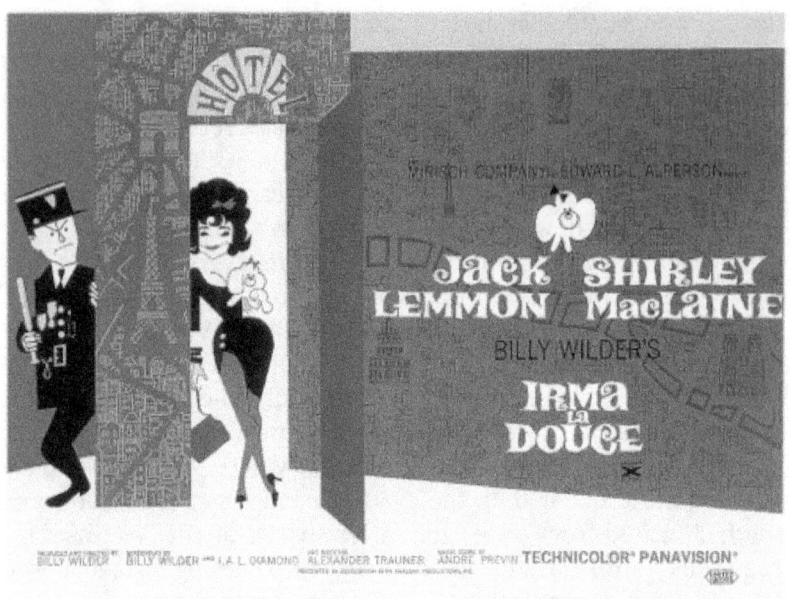

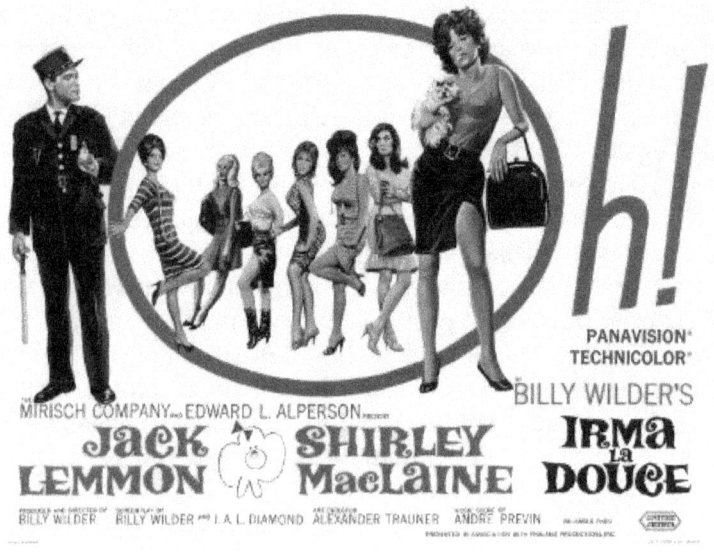

Tura's first poster, but she's still in the background.

Irma la Douce
(1963)

Director: Billy Wilder
Writers: Billy Wilder and I A L Diamond, from the play by
Alexandre Breffort
Stars: Jack Lemmon and Shirley Maclaine

The first time I saw *Irma la Douce*, I was watching anything by
Billy Wilder that I could find. My DVR was misbehaving and it
stuttered its way through the second half of the film so badly that it
was hard to see anything at all. It was Billy Wilder though, so I owed
it to myself to see it. This time out, I had a decent quality copy but I
was watching for Tura Satana, who died a year earlier and is sorely
missed. Her impact on film can't be underestimated, even though
she only made ten pictures over almost fifty years and four of those
were for Ted V Mikels, hardly a Billy Wilder.

This was her debut on the big screen, as it was for James Caan,
and she reached the second page of credits. That's one page ahead
of Bill Bixby. She even gets a few lines as Suzette Wong, hardly an
inspired name but an appropriate one nonetheless for an Asian
prostitute in Paris. I'm not going to complain about seeing Tura in
purple underwear but her eyeshadow is scary. She doesn't quite
look herself.

She's not the only source of colour here. We begin by zooming in
on the title character, another Parisian prostitute played by Shirley
Maclaine who stakes out her territory on Rue Casanova in
outrageous lime green, which is mirrored in the opening credits.
Irma is more talented than most of her colleagues, though she's as
professionally detached as they come. She can really sway up the
Hotel Casanova staircase and she can spin a sob story like nobody's
business to ensure that her marks leave plentiful tips beyond her
basic fee.

All her sisters of the street are colourful, which highlights just
how colourful Nestor Patou isn't when he shows up dressed all in
black. He's that rarest of beasts in Paris, an honest cop, newly
promoted from a children's playground and working his first day

on the beat. The only colour he has is in his experience: he's so green that he doesn't even know the number for the police station and he double takes what he sees on Rue Casanova. "Something tells me they're streetwalkers," he confides in Irma, who he only half believes isn't just walking her little dog. So he raids the Hotel Casanova and ships off the ladies of the evening, all sixteen of them, to jail.

Now, Nestor Patou is played by Jack Lemmon, who shares top billing with Shirley Maclaine. This was a reunion for them, having been so successful together in *The Apartment* three years earlier, also for Billy Wilder. In fact, Maclaine signed on without even reading the script, simply because she "believed in Wilder and Lemmon." She wasn't happy with the end product, which she regarded as "crude and clumsy," even if it did garner her a third Oscar nomination; she didn't win until her sixth, twenty years later for *Terms of Endearment*. So when Patou is promptly fired from the force for not realising that one of the johns he busted was his own boss, we know he isn't going to leave the story and in fact the real story is about to begin.

Irma la Douce was sourced from a French musical, hence the salacious subject matter which isn't what you might expect from Hollywood during the era of the puritanical Production Code. It was first staged in 1956, successfully enough to cross the channel to the West End in London and finally reaching Broadway, where it won Elizabeth Seal a Tony, in 1961. Never able to overlook successful stage material, Hollywood optioned it but surprisingly turned it into a straight comedy. Wilder was apparently uncomfortable with singing and dancing numbers, but he did allow André Previn to fill the film with music, enough so that it won an Oscar for its score. I'm happy for the changed approach, not only because I'm not a fan of musicals but because Wilder's comedic touch is the biggest success here. Perhaps because he could write comedy, he was also able to shoot it; though he made dramatic films as great as *Double Indemnity*, *Sunset Boulevard* and *The Lost Weekend*, it's comedies like *The Apartment* and *Some Like It Hot* that define him.

This one isn't up to those standards but it has much to be remembered for. Most obvious is the performance of Jack Lemmon. The central thrust of the story, if such a term can be used in a film about prostitution, is that Nestor Patou inadvertently becomes Irma's pimp and lover, though he never approves of her work. Unable to talk her out of her job or into allowing him to work to keep her, he masquerades as a rich English lord who pays enough that she doesn't have to work for anyone else. To keep up this charade, he works multiple jobs on the sly while Irma is asleep. You can imagine the situation comedy wrought from the inability to sustain such a double life. Lord X is a construct of every British film Patou has ever seen and Lemmon's Terry-Thomas in an eye patch approach is at once contagious, irresistible and utterly ludicrous, pieced together from patches of cinematic cloth ripped from *Gunga Din*, *The Guns of Navarone*, *Bridge on the River Kwai*, even *Mutiny on the Bounty*.

The biggest flaw ties to Wilder's strong conviction that Jack Lemmon could do no wrong. It wouldn't have hurt to restrain his star a little here and it certainly wouldn't have hurt to build up some of the other characters in the film, especially Maclaine's. Writing in her memoir, *My Lucky Stars*, about Lemmon and *The Apartment*, she hints that Wilder didn't see her talent, and by extension, anyone else's, quite as much as he saw Lemmon's, and that reads very true here too.

The film is named for her character rather than his but he's focused on so strongly that it really should have been retitled *Nestor Patou*. Few others get a chance to shine, though Maclaine is impeccable in a rôle meant for Marilyn Monroe, who died before production began. Wilder's first choice was Elizabeth Taylor but he didn't want the drama that came with the Taylor/Burton affair ongoing at the time. Best of the rest is Lou Jacobi as Moustache, taking Charles Laughton's place after his death.

In fact, I probably appreciated Moustache more than any other character in this film. Instead of it taking its name from him, he takes his name from Chez Moustache, the bar that he owns and runs and which serves as both the base of operations for the local pimps and the local hangout for their girls. More than anyone else, we want to know more about him. We hear all sorts of stories about his background and while it's unlikely that any of them are true, we do so want them to be. Certainly he's the most grounded character in the story, he's inevitably behind whatever transpires and he imparts a good deal of the homespun philosophy of the film. That guarantees that he also gets a good proportion of the best lines. "It's a hard way to make an easy living," Moustache tells a rapidly tiring Nestor. His character is a real gem, worthy of spinning off into other films and situations. I'm sure the reason for Jacobi's delivery being so consistently spot on is his background as a stand up comedian, but that's another story.

Beyond more Moustache, I wanted to see more of the colours and textures of the Rue Casanova set that cost $350,000 in 1963 money to build, but they're also glossed over for the most part. We have to settle instead for colourful names and a few scenes or lines here and there to offer hints of what might have been.

Of Irma's fellow prostitutes, Hope Holiday gets most screen time as Lolita, but she was the least interesting to me and the most annoying with her heart shaped sunglasses and her squeaky voice. I wanted to learn more about Mimi the MauMau, Kiki the Cossack and the Zebra twins, not to mention Suzette Wong. Tura Satana ends up with a surprising amount of screen time for her debut feature, though most of it is unfortunately only as background. She has big hair and lots of make up, as well as a variety of outfits with tassels that hint at her regular work as an exotic dancer. Her best scene is the raid, where she looks happy. Most of her screen rôles didn't call for that quality, as she was so good at playing the villain, or at least the anti-hero. I shouldn't call her a heroine here, as she's someone who sells her body for money, but the prostitutes in this film are seen a lot more positively than the Breen Office probably would have liked.

I wanted to learn about their equally colourfully named pimps too, like One Armed JoJo, Casablanca Charlie and Hippolyte the Ox, from whom Nestor won Irma in a truly bizarre fight scene that has to be seen to be believed. It's not quite slapstick but it's closer to that than any other fighting style. Regardless of the imaginative use of props, it's much more Buster Keaton than Jackie Chan.

In keeping with the live and let live attitude of the cops that's detailed at the beginning of the film by the narrator, we see very little of law enforcement. I wouldn't have minded more about that narrator too, who works in the stomach of Paris and who speaks with the uncredited but memorable voice of Louis Jourdan. After all, he's our guide to this story and the city in which it unfolds and he isn't given appropriate opportunity to live up to more than a little of that responsibility.

In the end, though, we don't get much more Jourdan, much more of the pimps or even much more of the girls, though it's not often that they're too far away from decorating another scene. What we get is much more Jack Lemmon.

Now, the good news is that lots of Jack Lemmon is hardly a bad consolation prize, especially when he's working for Billy Wilder, who cast him in seven of his films, including *Some Like It Hot* and *The Apartment*, two of the greatest comedies Hollywood ever made.

The bad news is that after that pinnacle, each of Wilder's pictures seemed a little less remarkable and this was the beginning of that downward slope. Wilder didn't translate well to the seventies at all, but he was still watchable and it's not unfair to suggest that lesser Lemmon and Wilder is still a good deal better than the best most filmmakers can come up with. This still feels like classic era stuff and it's an enjoyable picture but, as with *One, Two, Three*, his Jimmy Cagney movie a year earlier, the cracks were beginning to show. Once you've seen enough of his truly classic pictures, it won't be a stretch for you to see what this one could have been but wasn't.

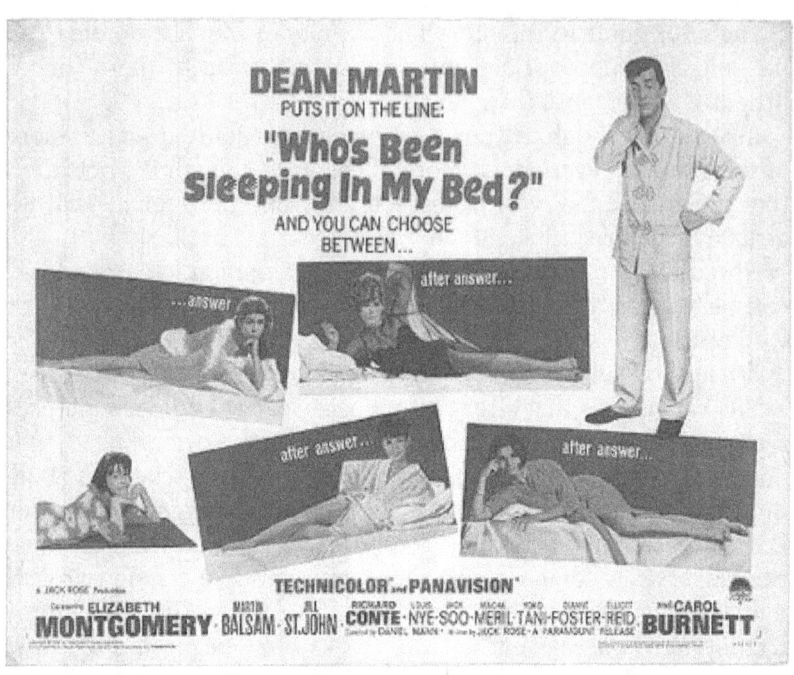

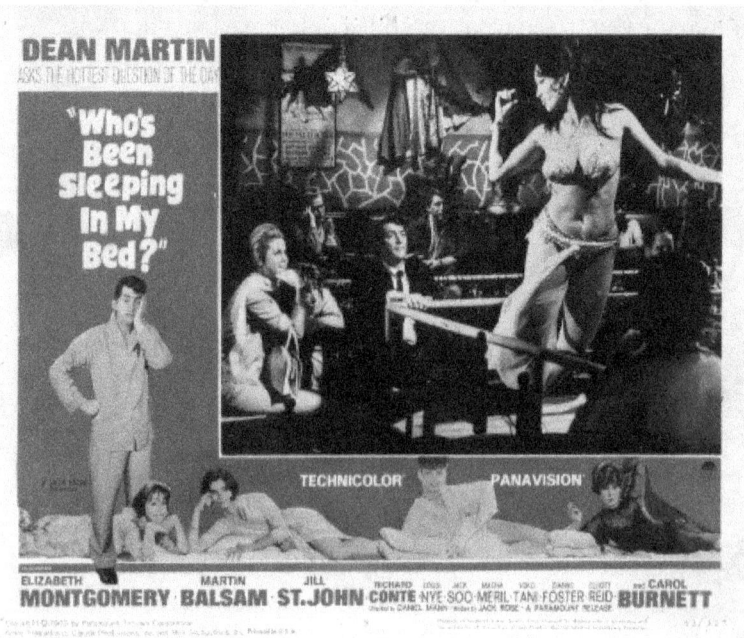

Who's Been Sleeping in My Bed? (1963)

Director: Daniel Mann
Writer: Jack Rose
Stars: Dean Martin, Elizabeth Montgomery and Carol Burnett

Tura Satana made two films for director Daniel Mann, which means one more than she made for Russ Meyer, with whom she's forever associated. In fact, given that her fifty year career totalled only ten films in all, that means that Mann made a full twenty percent of her films, and yet she played an uncredited stripper in both of them. That's a shame.

It's also a shame that this one doesn't remotely live up to its potential, especially as it had such a promising outline. Made the same year as *Irma la Douce*, it's a vehicle for Dean Martin, who coincidentally starred in Billy Wilder's next film, *Kiss Me, Stupid*, and it's a great multilayered part for him, given that he doesn't just get to play actor Jason Steel but the character that Jason Steel plays on television too, the apparently flawless title rôle in *Ask Dr Adam*. That's not a bad deal really, but the problem is that the ladies in the story see him more as Dr Adam than they do Jason Steel and, as they say, hilarity ensues.

The similarities between Steel and Adam are highlighted early, which is promising. "There's a lot more to being a doctor than checking thermometers and taking pulses," a nurse tells him as he saves a marriage. "It's all in a day's work," Adam replies and walks off into the credits, to emerge in the car park as Steel to rail at the godlike status of his character and cycle off into the sunset: two exit scenes running, so we can't help but compare them.

He's grouchy because he's about to get married, though he's enough of a man's man to still maintain a cool bachelor pad with a enviably spacious bar and a gentleman's gentleman of his very own. Glenn Quagmire would be proud. Steel is nervous but not with cold feet. If he had his way, he'd elope right away and avoid the big wedding, his immediacy understandable when you realise that his fiancée is an art teacher played by Elizabeth Montgomery. He might have managed it too had they been the only characters to watch, but no, he has five unhappily married poker buddies.

These misogynists want nothing more than to escape their wives and play poker together every Wednesday night, while their better halves try everything they can to stop them. Why, I have no idea, given that these gents are hardly likely to be good company if the girls met with success.

Tom Edwards doesn't want to celebrate his fifth wedding anniversary with his French wife. "Let's not be slaves to this middle class nonsense," he tells her. "It's just another day on the calendar." He can resist her delightful accent, though I'm not sure how. Harry Tobler has had two heart attacks already, dancing with his supple wife, and he doesn't want another one, but I'd certainly chance it. Yoshimi Hiroti doesn't want the traditional Japanese culture his wife smothers him with; I'd take it all. Sanford Kaufman wants out of a lecture on pre-Columbian art his wife wants to drag him along to; actually, I'd go for that too. Only Leonard Ashley's wife practices reverse psychology, making him feel as thoroughly guilty as she can. She'd let him kill her if it'll only make him happy. Now, there I'd draw the line.

And so the neglected wives start to ring Dr Adam at the poker game because, hey, he can do it all: fix medical ailments on the operating table and human problems away from it. They see Jason as the character he plays on television so much that they start calling him Doctor. Thus Jason starts to experience married life by proxy, his decent, easy going nature taken advantage of by a bevy of beauties desperate for attention.

So Jacqueline Edwards cooks for him, Toby Tobler dances with him and Isami Tani sings to him while walking over his back, all of them unloading their troubles at the same time. You can imagine how easily this leads to situation comedy, with Steel struggling to keep all these ladies apart, but it also leads to breakdown as Mona Kaufman rings him to complain about her husband right after he's booked himself in to see him the next day at his practice. Sanford is a psychiatrist as well as a poker buddy.

I really enjoyed the film up to this point, but here's where it begins to drift downhill. That's not to say it's been without flaws thus far. It's a particularly testosterone fuelled romance, perhaps the true opposite of a chick flick, with the misogyny inherent rather than confined to the misogynistic husbands. The moral really feels like these guys have the right attitude. Sure, they each made the same mistake and got married, but that's all behind them now. They've woken up, smelled the coffee and come to terms with it. They can deal with the little ladies back home well enough, or so they think, and we're supposed to hope that Jason Steel learns their lessons in time to avoid making the same mistake himself. No, that's hardly how it turns out in the end, of course, but Hollywood always had a habit of throwing in endings to satisfy certain audiences, whether they be female filmgoers who flocked to see Dean Martin movies or administrators of the Production Code who were all about having the sanctity of marriage firmly underlined on the big screen.

This attitude is dominant partly because every one of the female characters is so poorly written. Elizabeth Montgomery got a co-starring credit as Steel's intended, Melissa Morris, and you'd think she'd be important, but she's hardly in the movie at all. Even when she's given screen time, she gets a lot less to do with it than does Carol Burnett, who stamps all over her scenes as if she owned them. Then again, Montgomery is only a highly recognisable face to us today because of *Bewitched*, which didn't begin until the year after this film. While Burnett was debuting on the big screen here, she was already a household name on television, 1963 marking her second consecutive Emmy, the first for *The Garry Moore Show* and the second for both *Julie and Carol at Carnegie Hall* and *An Evening with Carol Burnett*. She pulls out the stops here and gets most of the best lines of the picture but, frankly, I'd much rather have seen more of Montgomery. Burnett is annoying here, Montgomery isn't.

As for the other women, they don't get much to do either except provide potential validation as to why their husbands don't want to spend time with them any more. They may be delightful to look at, as you might expect from actresses like Jill St John, Macha Méril and Yoko Tani, and they sound perfectly delightful on paper but in reality they're all clingy and whiny and not remotely grounded. They may entertain us, but they drive poor Jason Steel batty. Like Montgomery, they also disappear mostly into the background as the capable, if predictable, comedy of the first half deteriorates into silliness and slapstick in the second half as Carol Burnett takes over and Dean Martin runs wild.

This latter is at least a saving grace, given that Dino gets to try out a Cary Grant impersonation at one point and even a couple of Dean Martin impressions too, which are somehow appropriate for a picture in which he plays a character who plays another character. It's only fair to have his character play him too.

The most interesting thing with the script is how it moves in two opposite directions at the same time. As Jason Steel finds himself unwittingly helping out everyone else's marriage by doing very little except being nice, he feels increasingly afraid of beginning his own. His session with Dr Kaufman is surely enough to define him as a confirmed bachelor. Yet, as the ladies treat him more and more like the perfect character he plays on TV, he becomes less and less perfect himself, becoming unstable to the point where we wonder why our delightful art teacher still wants him.

It's hardly as if these two actors weren't accustomed to ending marriages. Montgomery had already divorced two husbands and she married her third while making this film. While that marriage would also end in divorce, it also produced her three children and her abiding fame, as that third husband was William Asher, who promptly produced and directed her in Bewitched. Dino also went through three divorces but at this point was fourteen years into the twenty three which his second marriage would last, one that would coincidentally also give him three children.

It's hard to see how this film could have been fixed. The premise is a good one and I'm hardly going to complain about the stellar cast, but it seems to consistently take the wrong direction at every step. For a while those wrong directions are still funny, so we can run with it, writer Jack Rose being no rookie with a pair of Oscar nominations, for The Seven Little Foys and Houseboat, behind him and a third for A Touch of Class still to come. However by the halfway point all the bad directions have only set up more bad directions and the humour drains out of them as situations progress.

At almost an hour and three quarters, it's also too long. One of the few second half highlights is that uncredited performance by Tura Satana, who's given a brief spot as a stripper in a Tijuana bar, moving a heck of a lot more than she ever got a chance to do in

Irma la Douce. She sure was flexible back then, hardly surprising as she'd been a successful exotic dancer for years. Acting at this point was a step into a possible future, perhaps prompted by words of Harold Lloyd, for whom she'd been a nude model. "The camera loves your face," he told her. "You should be seen." It's a shame that her work on this film was seen mostly in the choreography she designed for Carol Burnett.

If only the script had been as flexible as Tura, as it would perhaps have given us a lot more to enjoy from the perspective of a notably different era.

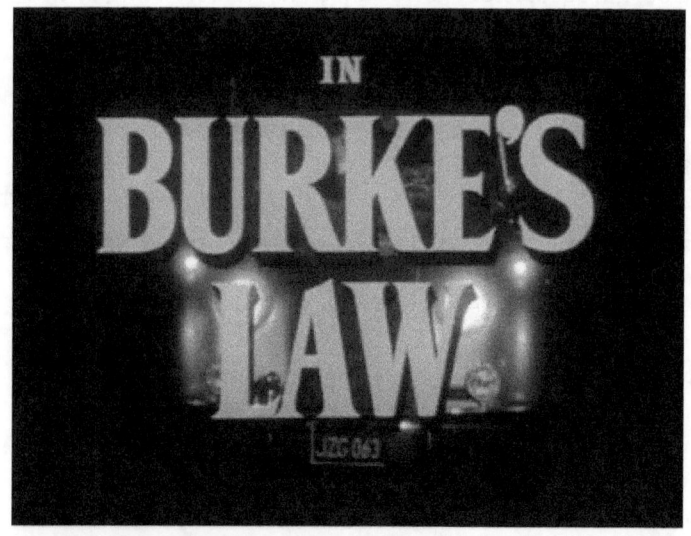

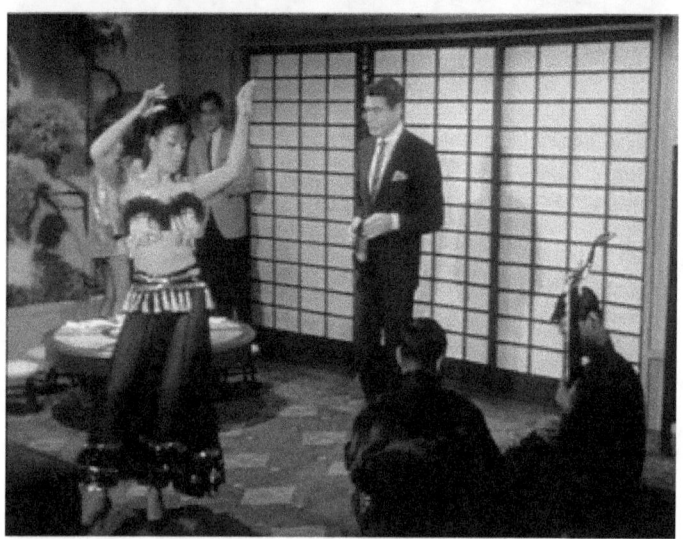

Tura dancing at the Paper Dragon in front of Capt Amos Burke.

Burke's Law:
Who Killed the Paper Dragon?
(1964)

Director: Marc Daniels
Writers: Jameson Brewer & Day Keene
Star: Gene Barry

I find it fascinating to watch old TV shows that are completely new to me, far more than revisiting ones I have memories of. Like most kids who grew up in the seventies and eighties, television was a frequent background, but going back to shows I enjoyed when I was young tends to provide a mixed experience. For every guilty pleasure which turns out to remain surprisingly entertaining, such as *The Dukes of Hazzard*, there's a show that makes me cringe with how awful it really was, such as *The Fall Guy*.

I'd never seen *Burke's Law*, so *Who Killed the Paper Dragon?*, the 25th of 32 episodes in the first of two regular seasons, was a new experience for me, though the actors were familiar faces, from the star through most of the regulars to the substantial and impressive guest cast. These particular guest stars and the background that unfolds against oriental culture are likely to make this one a favourite episode, but based on this episode, I'd expect to enjoy this show generally.

Amos Burke is an unlikely character, somehow both an insightful captain in the homicide division of the LAPD and a millionaire, who eschews a traditional police car for a Rolls Royce Silver Cloud and a chauffeur. He was played by Gene Barry, who spun a recurring character in a sitcom called *Our Miss Brooks*, starring Eve Arden, into three leading roles on major shows over the next fifteen years; *Burke's Law* was the middle of the three, following *Bat Masterson* but predating *The Name of the Game*. Though the tone and genre was different across each series, he was a rich ladies man in all of them. Probably most famous today for playing the lead in the George Pal version of *The War of the Worlds* in 1953, I remember him just as well from movies for Sam Fuller and William Castle and will now add his TV work to those memories. He's obviously an endearing television lead, someone who can elevate fluff into something apparently more substantial and prompt us to return a week later for more.

For this episode of *Burke's Law*, we're in Chinatown during New Year celebrations, clearly just an excuse to show us fireworks and dragon dancers. It's capably shot and neatly edited, providing a surprising amount of local colour for a black and white show.

Into these celebrations ploughs a Triumph; its lady driver and a young girl promptly vanish into the crowd. As onlookers surround the busted vehicle, an annoying schoolteacher from Oklahoma sees the corpse in the boot, so Burke and his team are promptly called in to investigate. He's already in his Rolls, smooching in the back seat with a vapid, if not half sedated, blonde Barbie in a tiara; his men are there as he arrives, stuck firmly in the limited scopes of their characters. Det Tim Tilson is a hotshot assistant, who quickly racks up all the facts, but apparently never discovers whodunit before Burke. More experienced is Sgt Les Hart, who is still just another background prop for Burke to bounce off.

As we're in Chinatown and the victim is a professor of Oriental Philosophy, Eric Hanson by name, you can be sure that writers Jameson Brewer and Day Keene threw everything they could imagine from Asian culture into the mix.

The central location for the story is the Paper Dragon, a Chinese restaurant at which the car's driver works as a dancer. Almost immediately, the usual stereotypes leap into play, though they're surprisingly alternately embraced and debunked throughout the episode. The first instance, with Burke swapping self deprecating high Chinese platitudes with smalltime wheeler dealer Sidney Ying, is instantly painfully stereotypical, though both characters switch over to regular English soon enough. Even then, Ying has to throw a cheap line of dialogue sourced from mixed cultures and Burke has to throw back, "Any Chinese who would say that ought to be ashamed of himself." This sort of thing continues throughout, with us cringing, then laughing, then wondering.

What's most shocking is that Ying is played by James Shigeta, very possibly the last actor I'd have expected to see spouting Oriental clichés at this point. He was a third generation American, born in Hawaii from Japanese heritage. He broke important ground in his debut feature, as a third of an interracial love triangle in Sam

Fuller's *The Crimson Kimono* in 1959. His next film cast him as the Chinese sidekick to an old West cowboy who fights racism after freeing a Chinese slave and falling for her. His biggest rôle was in 1961, when he landed the lead in the big screen adaptation of the hit Rodgers and Hammerstein musical, *Flower Drum Song*; by this point, he was the closest thing to an Asian star in America since the silent films of Sessue Hayakawa and Anna May Wong. While his character does evolve here and it's far from all bad, it's still galling to find an actor with this much background spouting lines like, "Yikes, I've been talking with dishonourable fuzz."

This scene is also Tura Satana's scene. We see her on a dancefloor as Burke walks in, leaning over backwards so far that her hair almost touches the floor. It's a subdued dance for her, much more traditionally feminine than usual, though when she starts to steal the scene by literally dancing her way around Burke and Ying's deteriorating conversation, her animalistic power is still obvious and she finishes it as a whirling dervish. She only gets one line, which fortunately has value, and then she's gone from the episode.

However low down the credits list she got, which was low enough that she wasn't one of the six guest stars for the episode, she still got more dancing time than Lotus Bud, her fellow dancer at the Paper Dragon and the prime suspect in Prof Hanson's murder. Lotus Bud, the moonlighting name of Mary Ling, the professor's assistant, is played by Miyoshi Umeki, the first Asian actor to win an Oscar, for *Sayonara* in 1957. She also acted alongside Shigeta in *Flower Drum Song*.

However cheesy and stereotypical the script gets, this episode deserves praise for its stellar cast of Asian actors, who are treated well for the most part: seen not only as Asian characters, but as people, good and bad and in between. Beyond Shigeta and Umeki, there's also Ginny Tiu, a child prodigy on the piano who at only ten years of age was still an old hand on television, having debuted on *The Ed Sullivan Show* at five. She was prominent enough to have already been given the enviable (or unenviable) choice of being in an Elvis Presley movie, *Girls! Girls! Girls!*, or to perform for John F Kennedy. For the record, she chose the King over the president.

Yet for a story all about Chinatown, not one of these actors is Chinese. Tiu was born in the Philippines of Hong Kong heritage,

Shigeta is American, Satana and Umeki were both Japanese by birth and Leon Lontoc, the sole Asian regular on the show as Henry, Burke's chauffeur, was another Filipino. While unacceptable to a purist, all of them are fine as generic Chinese characters.

Unfortunately, the final Chinese character is as far from fine as could be. For some inexplicable reason, though it was probably that it just seemed like a good punchline at the time, the owner of the Paper Dragon is played by Dan Duryea, perennial Hollywood villain. He's not his usual scoundrel here, but he's not his usual anything else either as the Cantonese/Irish Hop Sing Kelly, whose mixed heritage is riffed upon more than once. Like Shigeta's, Duryea's performance begins offensively and then progresses into laughter, but unlike Sidney Ying, Hop Sing Kelly promptly falls back into a realisation that Duryea managed to racially offend two completely different ethnicities in one fell swoop.

Fortunately the other two American guest stars are far more enjoyable: Howard Duff plays a good-hearted drunkard and "radio ventriloquist" called Charlie January, who had saved Lotus Bud's life during the war and now owns a responsibility for her wellbeing, and Barbara Eden as Prof Hanson's fresh widow, Sylvia. She's as delicious as always, but she's also deliciously drunk and spouting deliciously spiritualistic mumbo jumbo in the process.

Eden stood out for me in this episode, not merely because she always has a knack of turning me to jelly with the promises in her eyes, face and smile, but because she begins this episode cross legged on the bed looking rather Jeannie-ish, even though this is a full year before the beginning of *I Dream of Jeannie*. Everything I've read suggests that to compete with ABC's *Bewitched* in the ratings, NBC created that show from elements of *The Brass Bottle*, a 1964 movie about a djinn in which Eden starred, albeit not as a genie that time. The general concept and the casting choice may well have sprung from that picture, but surely her look here was a major influence too. She's shy of the headgear and her hair is up, but the bare belly, pose and harem style costume are far too close to be coincidence. She even drinks gin, as if time travelling scriptwriters threw in a pun just to make us wonder about synchronicity in the universe.

Given that I'm watching for Tura Satana, who gets one scene, it seems somehow appropriate that I'm far more interested in the guest stars in this episode than the regulars.

Beyond Gene Barry, who has fun burying himself in the setting to the degree that he finds a way to impersonate both Confucius and Charlie Chan, I recognised his co-stars too. Gary Conway plays Det Tilson like a future lead, which he soon became as *Land of the Giants* began in 1968, three years after the end of *Burke's Law*. Sgt Hart is down to earth Regis Toomey, a regular Hollywood face whose 182 credits (and I'm talking only films here, not counting his prolific TV work) spanned seven decades from the poor Roland West movie, *Alibi*, in 1929, through a particularly strong decade in the forties to *Evil Town*, a horror movie mostly shot in the seventies but not released until 1987.

Yet this is an opportunity not for them but for Shigeta, Eden, Duff and Tiu. Even Tura Satana with her one scene is far more noticeable here than most of the regulars. As I soon found with her other work for television, at this point regulars appear to have been the riffs that shows reused while the guest stars were the solos.

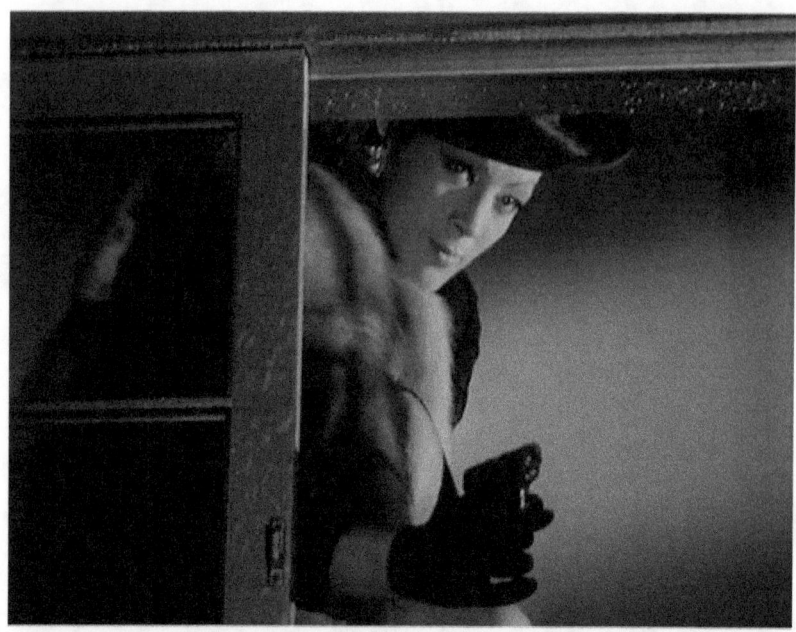

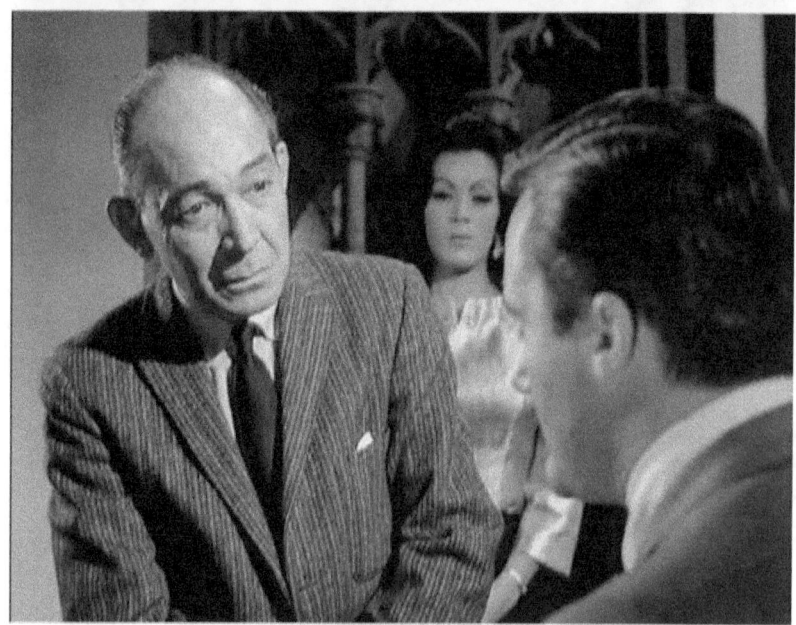

Tura watching an interrogation with a quiet air of menace.

The Man from UNCLE:
The Finny Foot Affair
(1964)

Director: Marc Daniels
Writers: Jack Turley and Jay Simms
Stars: Robert Vaughan, David MacCallum and Leo G Carroll

While I'd never seen *Burke's Law* before, I'd grown up with *The Man from UNCLE*. To be fair, I read a lot more of the books than I ever saw episodes of the TV show, but I knew the formula well.

The Finny Foot Affair was only the tenth episode of the first season, so it was shot in black and white with Robert Vaughn emphatically the lead as international superspy and UNCLE agent, Napoleon Solo. Producer Norman Felton wanted a spy series in the vein of Hitchcock's *North by Northwest*, so he worked with James Bond creator Ian Fleming to build the formula that paired Solo, a suave Cary Grant type, with a different innocent character each episode who had been inadvertently caught up in the story. Here, that's a thirteen year old Kurt Russell. Illya Kuryakin, Solo's Russian sidekick throughout the show's run, wouldn't find prominence until episode 20, elevated because the enigmatic David McCallum became a surprise sex symbol with the young ladies who watched *The Man from UNCLE*. He's hardly in this episode.

Initially it plays out like a science fiction show. Solo and Kuryakin land an UNCLE helicopter on an island off the coast of Scotland, put on something resembling space helmets and wander through a dead town. The stark black and white pairs with the uncanny quiet to give an otherwordly feel. What few people we see are dead in the street, though the actors aren't good at being corpses, breathing and fluttering their eyelids a little too much. After loading up a crate found outside Dr McDonald's practice with the label, "To highest authority. Open only under controlled conditions," they toss a couple of incendiary grenades into a conveniently large stack of flammable material and so torch the town. What they return to HQ turns out to be a seal, one that is unquestionably young but which died old after eating a last meal of blue gilled sardines that are only found off the coast of Norway. Those plot conveniences in modern forensic crime shows really aren't new, folks.

Of course someone in this deserted town saw them take off again, because you can't have a spy organisation fighting for the good of mankind without some sort of villainous equivalent. The villains here are a little more ambiguous than usual, but they're led by a Japanese general named Yokura, who's leading a team to locate a mysterious concoction called Formula J47 from his base in a castle on the Norwegian coast.

He's played by Leonard Strong, an American actor who wasn't of Asian heritage but whose elusive looks allowed him to specialise in playing Asian characters anyway. It's amusing to hear his heavily accented English while his number two, played by Japanese born Tura Satana, is far less stereotypical. She's Tomo and she takes care of business for him. "Go to London," he tells her. "Be my eyes." Unfortunately she doesn't get to be much more than his eyes, his ears and his word, but she does hint frequently at being his fists, exhibiting if not unleashing the raw power that she'd exhibit so magnificently only a year later in *Faster, Pussycat! Kill! Kill!*

Of all the general's entourage, she's the one who stands out. We first meet her dancing towards the camera in a flowing dress, as feminine as she was dancing in her episode of *Burke's Law*, but with even more substance to her. Just these few seconds is enough to highlight why she danced professionally under the billing of Galatea, the Statue that Came to Life. She remains both stylish and sinister as she and her cronies follow Solo and his inadvertent companion around from place to place, always carrying the edge of danger that none of those cronies manage to pull off. Later on, while Solo and Yakura chat, she stands to the side in her black trousers like a panther. All the other henchmen just stand there, even after Solo gets the upper hand, because the script hasn't anything for them to do. Yet Tomo is clearly ready for anything. She vibrates with pent up energy, like a spring about to explode. She's danger on two legs, a clear hint at what was to come.

In fact, the only scene in which she looks out of place is the one where she's pouring a glass of sake for the general. She's unsure and overly careful, obviously not good at deference. Luckily, in this episode the deference is all in the hands of Kurt Russell, who's unmistakeable even at only thirteen.

He was actually riding high in 1964 as the title character in *The Travels of Jaimie McPheeters*, now an obscure western with a cult following, but back then an important show spun out of a Pulitzer prize winning novel with breakthrough rôles not only for Russell but also for Charles Bronson and four of the Osmond brothers. Here, he plays Christopher Larson, a precocious boy who latches onto Solo at the airport in London with the goal of setting him up with his widowed mother. After changing his destination from New York to Bergen to give himself more of a chance, he becomes both a liability to continually get Solo into trouble and an opportunity to continually allow him to escape again. He has fun with his rôle.

And so it goes for quite a while, building capably with a level of imagination that would believably have hooked audiences at the time and which we can still appreciate in hindsight, even though the majority of it is relatively transparent. Everything we see has a purpose, presented as a puzzle piece whose place in the big picture will become apparent later. Some are relatively easy to figure out, like Chris's useless machine that could only be a distraction, while others are more cryptic like the last message of a murdered UNCLE agent in Norway that suggests to "marry the maiden" I found myself impressed at how well phrased it all was. Technically it's accomplished well beyond what might be expected, the lighting, editing and camera movements being solid if expected, few scenes elevated to classic noir but all of them consistently impressive. The pace is especially remarkable, measured and unrushed, but always with something new to move it forward.

I was surprised to find that *The Finny Foot Affair* was directed by Marc Daniels, who was also the director of *Who Killed the Paper Dragon?*, Tura Satana's episode of *Burke's Law*. Daniels was a prolific and important name in early American television, most notable for his direction of the pioneering first 38 episodes of *I Love Lucy*, starting in 1951. During that run, he and Karl Freund perfected the three camera concept that's still routine today in live television.

Daniels was a generation behind Freund, one of the legends of cinematography who had shot many of the great expressionist pictures in Germany in the twenties, such as *The Golem*, *The Last Laugh* and *Metropolis*. Emigrating to the United States, he shot

Dracula for Tod Browning, then moved up to direct *The Mummy* and *Mad Love* himself. It's not difficult to see how Freund's vast experience and technological innovation influenced Daniels, who in turn could impart his own wisdom about working in television.

I also wonder how involved Daniels got with casting choices, especially as it was definitely his recommendation to cast Vivian Vance as Ethel Mertz in *I Love Lucy*. Robert Vaughn was cast as Napoleon Solo based on his work on *The Lieutenant*, an episode of which Daniels had directed earlier in 1964. He'd go on to direct four episodes of *The Man from UNCLE*, the earliest being the fourth. Even more notable, the episode of *Burke's Law* in which he directed Tura Satana was the only one he made for that show, yet that and this are the only two television appearances that she made in 1964. It wouldn't appear to be much of a stretch to guess that when he saw a script calling for tough Japanese characters, he remembered the powerful and exotic dancer who he'd directed mere months earlier. The only catch is that Daniels would continue to be prolific on television but Tura wouldn't, only returning for an episode of *The Girl from Uncle* in 1967.

That's especially a shame here because she gets more dialogue in this 50 minute episode than in any of her films outside *Faster, Pussycat! Kill! Kill!* and her early Ted V Mikels pictures. If American TV in the sixties was all about the guest stars, she could have found a much more prominent niche there than in theatrical features. Beyond Robert Vaughn, who dominates this episode of *The Man from UNCLE*, and Kurt Russell, who is on screen for most of three of the four acts, she's the most obvious member of the cast.

She's more prominent than David McCallum, who would soon begin to get more fan mail than anyone else in the history of MGM television. She's far more watchable than Leonard Strong, whose routine was getting old while hers was becoming new. She certainly wasn't given enough opportunity here, but she still showed what she could do.

With hindsight, it serves as both a lost opportunity and a strong hint towards what she would shortly accomplish in *Faster, Pussycat! Kill! Kill!*

Velvet Glove Cast in Iron: The Films of Tura Satana

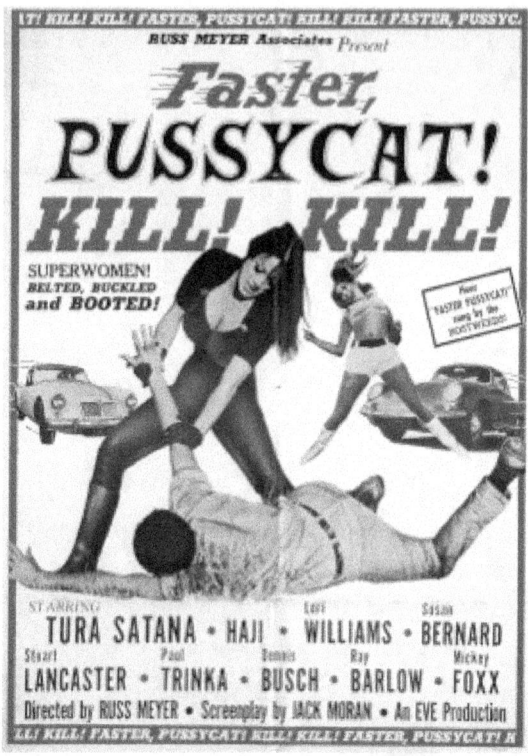

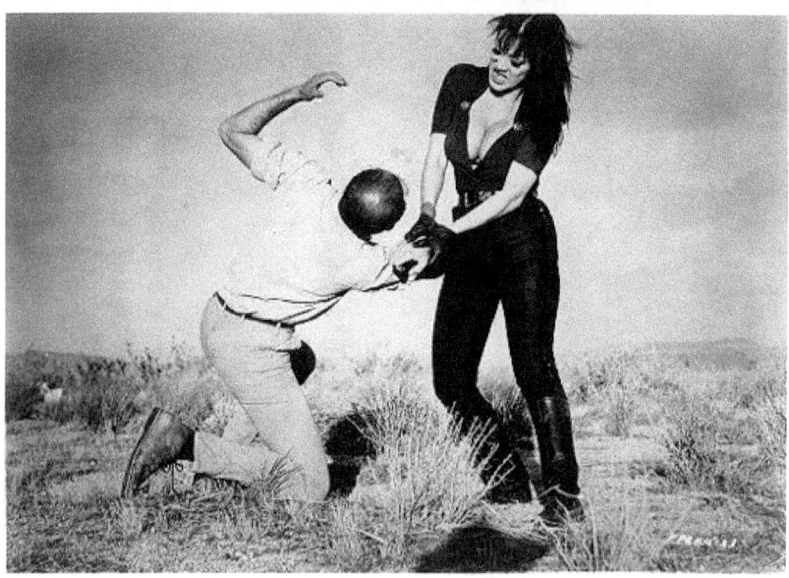

Faster, Pussycat! Kill! Kill! *(1965)*

Director: Russ Meyer
Writer: Jack Moran
Star: Tura Satana

What a difference two years can make. In 1963, Tura Satana was working in Hollywood. She had a few lines as a Parisian prostitute in a Billy Wilder picture, then, as an uncredited stripper, served as the exotic backdrop for a Tijuana scene in a Dean Martin vehicle. In 1965, she was back on the big screen but this time playing the lead in a black and white indie flick for renegade filmmaker Russ Meyer.

Not only is she the focus of the film this time round, rather than a distraction, the tone is utterly different. *Irma la Douce* may have been written around salacious subject matter, but so far around it that it assiduously avoids the sex that drives every one of its many characters. *Who's Been Sleeping in My Bed?* was notably misogynistic, a sad product of its time. Yet this is something of a manifesto for feminine power, so much so that with hindsight, we might well be excused for thinking that Satana should have been snapped up by Hollywood as the next big thing. In reality they were scared stiff of her.

Back in the sixties, American cinema was dominated by men and there were few good rôles for women on or off the camera, talents as strong as Bette Davis struggling to find material of substance and only Ida Lupino able to represent the fairer sex in the director's chair. Of course, it hasn't changed much today (just compare Hollywood's current output to that of modern French cinema, for instance) but it's better than it was. At least there's a strong indie scene, with a low cost of entry and a number of options for distribution. When this film came out, there were few indie filmmakers and they were mostly crooks.

Meyer was a rarity, an auteur with a strong vision, the ability to make movies and the contacts to get them seen. He was a glamour photographer with early *Playboy* centrefolds to his name, he shot production stills for Hollywood movies and he filmed combat footage for the US Army during World War II. Many colleagues from those worlds also worked on his films.

It's something of an irony that it took Russ Meyer to champion the power of women, as he's hardly the epitome of the feminist. His first films, like *The Immoral Mr Teas*, *Eve and the Handyman* and *Wild Gals of the Naked West* fall into the nudie cutie genre, while his later ones, like *Supervixens*, *Up!* and *Beneath the Valley of the Ultravixens* are unmistakable for their plentiful use of topless or naked women with impossibly large breasts. He's an exploitation filmmaker frequently described as sexist and there's much in his pictures that precludes him from being identified as a feminist. Yet, with a few of his mid-period black and white films and especially with *Faster, Pussycat! Kill! Kill!*, he was the brightest beacon of light, not for the equality of women but for the superiority of them, in the whole of American cinema. He equates sex with violence from the outset, putting that power firmly with "this new breed, encased and contained within the supple skin of woman."

Meyer had a type, certainly, but it went beyond huge breasts to a more buxom version of the old pinup standard, which is exemplified here by three otherwise different leading ladies: Tura Satana as Varla, an exotic Amazon with make up that enhances her cat like eyes; Haji, a continental vixen called Rosie with a strong accent; and Lori Williams as Billie, an all-American blonde. All three certainly know how to move, being supple and flexible dancers even in tight jeans that emphasise hips and waists as well as breasts. Perhaps most importantly, all three possess a wild and strong spirit apparent whether dancing in a go-go bar or racing sports cars in the Mojave desert, both of which they do in the opening scenes. It's far from accidental that one is a traditionally female rôle while the other is traditionally male, as this film is all about obliterating those boundaries. Meyer's women are as powerful as they choose to be, as dominant as Varla, as submissive as Rosie or as free as Billie.

The first twenty minutes are a cinematic textbook worthy of exploration. The introduction is avant garde, featuring a growing number of spectographs of the narrator's voice, before exploding into life in a go-go bar. Meyer's camera literally looks up to these three powerful leads, except when they're wrestling in the water or sand. He places them into traditionally exploitative settings like exotic dances and catfights while demonstrating that they're not being exploited, instead being in command of their own destinies.

They're above the world at large, whose pecking order is mirrored within the trio. Meyer quickly establishes their respective places: Varla clearly dominant, Rosie submissive to her and Billie wild enough to question but not tough enough to challenge. Compare them to Linda, a bouncy *Gidget* clone who doesn't get out of her boyfriend's car until after he leads the way. She's as weak as the others are strong, but she can't comprehend their threat, not just to her but her way of life.

Watching Linda and Tommy interact with Varla and the others is almost surreal; it's easy to read it in a much wider cinematic context than it was ever intended. Linda and Tommy are happy, polite and asexual, even with Linda in a bikini, only able to function within the confines of a strict set of rules, like the Production Code under which mainstream American film had been restricted since 1934. Yet Varla and her girls ooze defiance and sexuality with every word, move and action, reminiscent of the precodes or, more prophetically, the films that would kill the Production Code only a couple of years later and lead to the temporary creative freedom of the early seventies. Like the Code was doing at the time, Linda and Tommy are fighting a battle they can't win as don't understand what they're fighting. "Would you like a soft drink?" asks Linda, almost mindlessly happy. "We don't like nothing soft," replies Rosie. "Everything we do is hard." They're speaking a different language.

The most obvious new ground is set here too, namely Varla's murder of Tommy. Clean cut, with a cute girlfriend and an obsession with his car, which he tunes to perfection and races against the clock, Tommy is the epitome of the American boy. We don't need to be told that he was his high school's quarterback or that he was voted King of the Prom, we just know. Yet he's just as unable to deal with these strange new girls as Linda. "What's it mean if you don't beat anyone?" asks Varla and he actually tries to answer. His only defense is to not play her game, to retreat to his car and wait for reality to follow him. Unfortunately Linda presses him to race the girls. Temporarily in his element again, he succeeds, but then Varla changes the rules and runs him off the track. He's instantly lost again, unable to even leave his car until his damsel is in distress. Even then, Varla proves tougher than him. She leaves him dead on the sand and traditional American masculinity with him.

To be honest, the film could have ended there, with Varla snapping Tommy's neck, less than twenty minutes in, and critics like me would still have as much to say about it, but there's a story still to be told, sparked by a talkative gas station attendant. Out in the desert is a crippled old man, with a fortune stashed away on his property because he doesn't believe in banks, and Varla wants it all.

What she finds isn't quite what she expects. The old man is a twisted character with a whole slew of secrets beyond the location of the money. He lives with two sons, one a brain damaged muscle man, tastefully known as The Vegetable, and another who seems to be fighting his own battles in the household. The ambiguity of the characters is appreciated: not one of the good guys is entirely good and not one of the bad girls is entirely bad, so we have to find our own moral ground in the maelstrom of motivations that the story rolls on through like the trains that are so frequently referenced.

There are about a million reasons why this film shouldn't work. It's a broadly painted big picture with a few little portraits illustrated within it. The acting is far from accomplished, with Satana shouting most of her lines, Williams whispering most of hers and Haji's accent proving as elusive as it is wild. For all the new ground it breaks, it chooses not to explore other taboos, such as the obvious lesbian relationship between Varla and Rosie or the proclivities of the old man.

Yet it ably succeeds where greater films have failed, as it never loses the tension, danger and threat of violence that it starts with. Most of this is generated by Satana, who dominates effortlessly throughout. Rosie describes Varla as "a velvet glove cast in iron" and it's a fair description; as tough as she is, and Satana did all her own stunts and fight scenes, she's unmistakably female. The old man's description of her is "more stallion than man," again highlighting grace and power without masculinity.

This is perhaps Russ Meyer's greatest film and certainly his most remembered. It has all the great composition of frame that he's known for, given his background in still photography, and the same sort of dynamic editing which creates much of the motion in most of his films. One rare departure from the norm here is the use of a cinematographer, Walter Schenk, who also lensed *Mudhoney*, as Meyer tended to shoot his own films, in addition to writing, editing, producing, directing and, once home video became his biggest market, even answering the phone to take orders.

Yet, unsurprisingly, it isn't Meyer people remember most about this film, it's Tura Satana. While Meyer was able to move on to more films, finding new, ever more buxom, stars to showcase in ever more outlandish plots, Satana found it harder. Of course, film wasn't her primary medium to begin with, being a hugely successful exotic dancer, but Meyer isn't the only one to regret that he never cast her again.

Her rôle here wasn't restricted to the character she played on screen. She designed her own make up and costume; wrote or improvised some of her dialogue, including a few of the choicest lines in the film; and added real martial arts knowledge to her fight scenes. She had begun to learn aikido and karate after she was gang raped at the age of nine by five men, then spent fifteen years exacting her revenge. No wonder she was so believable and so relentlessly tough as Varla; she really was as relentlessly tough as Varla.

Whatever the provenance of the character, how much was written by Meyer and how much brought to the table by Satana, how much it's fictional and how much it's real, Varla is certainly one of the most abiding icons of exploitation cinema, so abiding that her influence has spread far beyond it. For a black and white 1965 indie film that cost a mere $45,000, *Faster, Pussycat! Kill! Kill!* continues to resonate today, as relevant as it ever was.

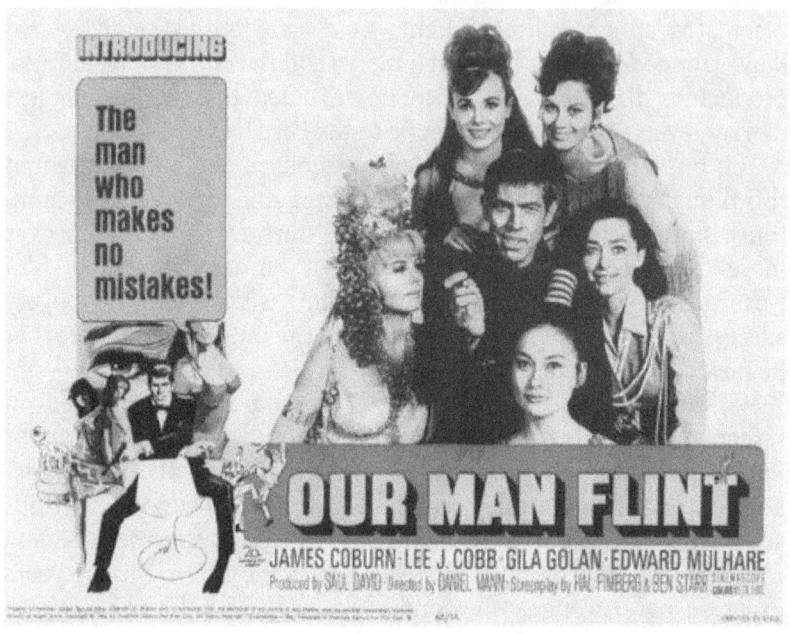

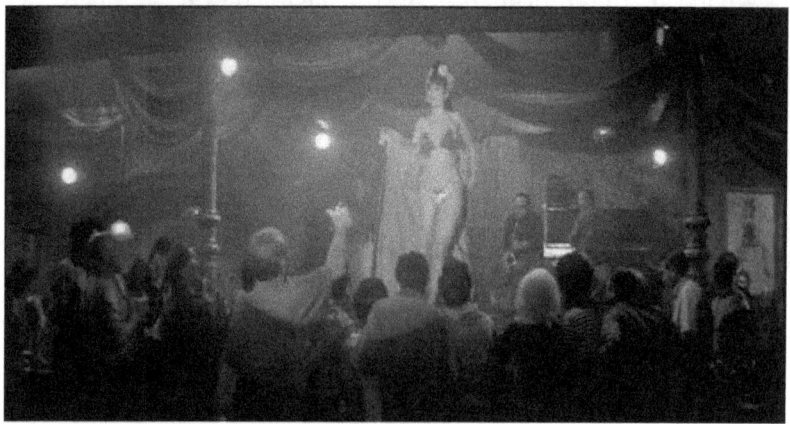

Tura is only ever visible in long shot in this film.

Our Man Flint
(1966)

Director: Daniel Mann
Writers: Hal Fimberg and Ben Starr
Stars: James Coburn, Lee J Cobb, Gila Golan and Edward Mulhare

Tura Satana made two films for director Daniel Mann, *Who's Been Sleeping in My Bed?* and *Our Man Flint*, and she played an uncredited stripper in both of them. The strange thing is that these two movies were separated by only three years in time but they were an era apart. In 1963, she was a burlesque dancer of note, an obvious choice to play a similar rôle on screen to spice up the background. By 1965, she was a great deal more than that: no less than the epitome of feminine power in film, courtesy of the picture she made in between, Russ Meyer's *Faster, Pussycat! Kill! Kill!*

Meyer regretted that she only made a single feature for him, but hindsight merely underlines how massively important she was in that one. It also puts these others into perspective and highlights the Hollywood mindset at the time. Good or bad, the mainstream films she appeared in have dated, often painfully, but Meyer's cheap indie film only gets better and more timely.

In many ways, *Our Man Flint* is the honest version of the others. *Irma la Douce* was ostensibly about a prostitute but Wilder's version turns it into a man saving her from herself. *Who's Been Sleeping in My Bed?* is a misogynistic romp that sets up Dean Martin as a bachelor supreme who marries only when his fiancée clearly demonstrates what she can do for him. At least *Our Man Flint* is honest in its sexism, creating in Derek Flint less of a James Bond spoof and more of a wish fulfilment version of what every American male dreamed of being: a man utterly in charge of his own destiny, who laughs at authority, achieves great physical and mental feats that literally save the world and, not remotely incidentally, maintains a bevy of gorgeous women at his beck and call. Yet Varla would eat them all for breakfast. "I never try anything; I just do it," she explains in *Faster, Pussycat! Kill! Kill!* and we believe her. Elvis Presley proposed to Tura. She turned him down. That's tough.

While Derek Flint isn't really a James Bond spoof, that doesn't mean that his film isn't. Director Daniel Mann suggested at the time that it was "a spoof on Douglas Fairbanks pictures" that involved "swashbuckling in modern dress". He may even have believed it, but Fairbanks was from another era and this was utterly of its time. It's absolutely a James Bond spoof, merely with Bond himself spun off into a peripheral character, named 0008 and with more than a passing resemblance to Sean Connery. He passes information to Flint during a fight scene at a strip club in Marseille. "It's bigger than SPECTRE," he tells him, "it's Galaxy." Coincidentally this is during Tura's performance. Later in the film, we see a character reading a 0008 book, another overt nod to the Bond series. So any pretense that this wasn't sending up Bond is ludicrous, it's simply that by relegating his equivalent to a minor rôle, Twentieth Century Fox inherently suggested their man is better.

They do more than suggest at the beginning of the film. A sinister organisation, which turns out to be Galaxy, is wreaking havoc globally by manipulating the weather: generating avalanches and hurricanes, triggering earthquakes and volcano eruptions, changing the global temperature at will. The bigwigs at ZOWIE (the Zonal Organisation World Intelligence Espionage) realise that their organisation has been infiltrated so they look outside for a saviour.

They throw punch cards into their UNIVAC and out pops the name of Derek Flint, regardless what source data or who enters it. He's the man for the job. Chief Cramden doesn't want to hire him, because he knows he doesn't take orders well, but he's overruled. Then we meet him: running through a martial arts kata and defeating all comers. Coburn obviously isn't Bruce Lee (though Lee would later train him), but he has a notable grin that hints at a good deal of character and a pristine air of supreme confidence.

Here's where he's firmly established as the wish fulfilment version of every male viewer. Not only ruggedly handsome and deft at martial arts, he's a renaissance man who gives Doc Savage a run for his money. He's an accomplished doctor, an antiques expert and a world class epicure. He's fluent in every language that arises. He can kill a fly with a blowdart, suspend himself between two chairs and stop his heart for three hours at a time. He's a master of improvisation. He's rich, of course. He has a penthouse apartment with talented guard dogs, a private jet and better equipment than ZOWIE: his cigarette lighter "has 82 different functions, 83 if you want to light a cigar." His quartet of international beauties take care of his every need. And he has the chutzpah to tell Cramden to get lost. The world can save itself without his help. It usually does. He's "the total man," the trailer calls him, "as much at home in the casbah as he is in the boudoir."

Of course he takes the job in the end, or otherwise we wouldn't have a film. He uses his unique talents to progress from exotic location to exotic location, exposing the good guys as idiots and tracking the bad guys to their lair.

His immediate foil is Gila, a ruthless agent for Galaxy who is as exotically beautiful as you might expect, actress Gila Golan not only being a runner up for Miss World, but Israeli via France and Poland. Needless to say she's extremely effective in everything she does, until Flint arrives on the scene and interrogates her in bed. I last saw her in 1969's *The Valley of Gwangi*, the last of the five films she made in the sixties, this being her second. After that she retired, to return to the big screen only once for a Italian football movie in 1984 that doesn't even have an English title. *Our Man Flint* saw her at the peak of her charm, but of course she's dominant only until the right man comes along, at which point she turns into putty in his hands.

Coburn and Golan are by far the most watchable characters. Lee J Cobb does a capable job as ZOWIE's Chief Cramden, just as the white labcoat clad scientists who lead Galaxy do capable jobs, but all of them are only really there as props for Flint.

Any way in which their actions seem topical is entirely accidental, such as the man made global warming that prompts panic amongst world leaders because they immediately see the damage it would cause. How realistic did that turn out to be? It was all utterly generic at the time, nothing more than hokey science fiction transplanted into a spy story, as was the norm. None of it makes the remotest sense, not that mad scientists are really supposed to make sense, but I've found over time that if you're going to ignore the laws of physics and tell a cartoon story, then at least go hog wild, especially with the style. Mario Bava's *Danger: Diabolik* was dumb but it stands up better today as entertainment than its more sophisticated peers.

Here, Galaxy's island headquarters in the Mediterranean is pretty cool but it can't hold a candle to Diabolik's underground secret lair. It's more notable for what it says about the writers, Hal Fimberg and Ben Starr, both best known otherwise for writing for television. Certainly this is as advertised as any home base of a secret terrorist organisation bent on world domination that I've ever seen. Not only do all the Galaxy henchmen wear uniforms, but the main building sports a logo. I loved the eagle that sits on the plinth outside it though. "An anti-American eagle," notes Flint. "That's diabolical."

This HQ looks roughly as you might expect, with art installations, industrial facilities and random numbers in coloured hexagons. Yet the island is a tropical paradise full of jugglers, folk musicians and bikini clad women wandering around apparently at random. It turns out that they're pleasure units, conditioned to provide bodily service to the men. That's not sexist, right?

But there I go, rationalising a spoof again. To be fair, it's easier here because *Our Man Flint* is a comedy that is played delightfully straight. The Austin Powers movies owe a lot to the Flint films, both this and its sequel, *In Like Flint*, which Powers reveals in *The Spy Who Shagged Me* to be his favourite movie. Yet they're overt comedies that couldn't be taken seriously if you tried. Flint is as outrageous in his way as Powers, yet he's no more unbelievable than the majority of the serious superspies who saved the world every ten minutes back in the sixties, that comment reflecting more on the supposedly serious characters than on Derek Flint.

This is a spoof that pokes fun at the spirit of the genre rather than its specifics, so there are no overt gags and few references to its targets. We're supposed to be thrilled more than set to laughter. While *Our Man Flint* is often a dated mess of a film, it and especially James Coburn still succeed on that front.

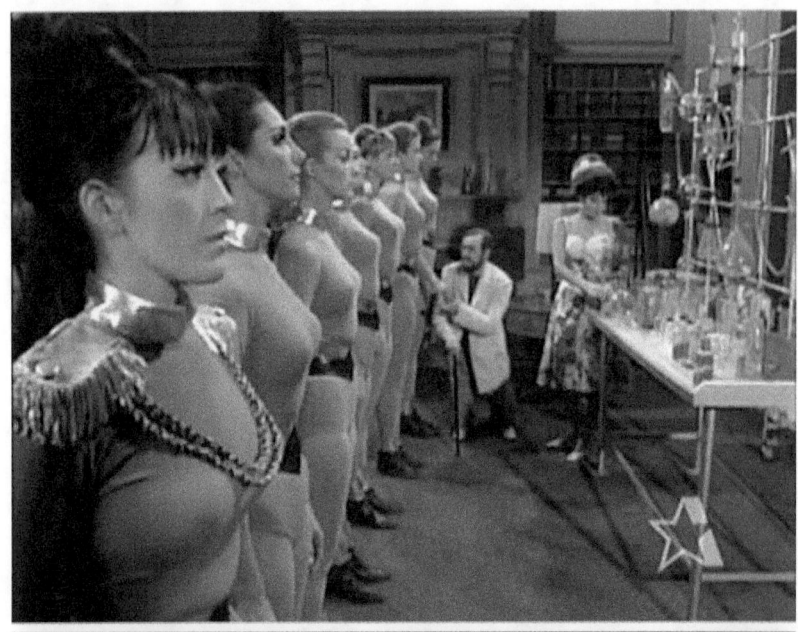

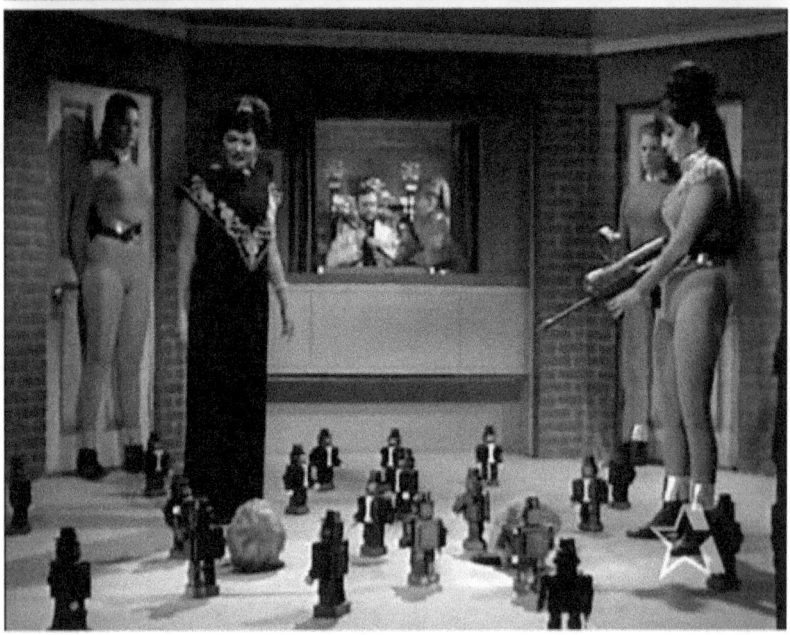

Yvonne De Carlo, Tura Satana and a game of exploding robot pinball.

The Girl from UNCLE:
The Moulin Ruse Affair
(1967)

Director: Barry Shear
Writers: Jay Simms and Fred Eggers, from a story by Jay Simms
Stars: Stefanie Powers and Noel Harrison

Three years after showing so much promise in an episode of *The Man from UNCLE*, Tura Satana returned to the UNCLE universe for its sister show, *The Girl from UNCLE*.

Unfortunately, although she plays the sort of character that she ought to rock, the leader of the villain's elite guard, she's given little opportunity to do so. She looks great, especially in a tight uniform with a stylish pair of epaulettes, and she's often on screen during the second half, but that's about it; she's tasked with simply looking great on screen, hardly a stretch for Tura in 1967.

It's no exaggeration to state that Tura Satana, Grandma Walton and a set of killer toy robots are the only positive things about this episode. The whole thing is so fundamentally awful that without background knowledge, it's difficult to imagine why anyone would greenlight this show and especially this particular episode. Well, there are reasons to be found, but *The Girl from UNCLE* was still inevitably dropped after a single season.

The first reason is that April Dancer, the titular girl from UNCLE who debuted in September 1966, was originally supposed to arrive with her male counterparts two years earlier, in September 1964. Producer Norman Felton had met with James Bond creator Ian Fleming to put together the concept design for a spy show that became *The Man from UNCLE*. Napoleon Solo was the original lead character in this design but Fleming also suggested a sultry secretary for his boss called April Dancer. Of course, it didn't happen, partly because the similarities to the James Bond series were quite obvious and Dancer was quite clearly a thinly veiled Miss Moneypenny, but the name never went away, being all ready to be used when a second reason showed up in January 1966 in the form of Adam West and Burt Ward. *The Man from UNCLE* had changed the face of American television, but only a year and half later, *Batman* did it again and stylish suspense gave way to camp comedy.

Needless to say, the two didn't mix well, but mix they did. *The Man from UNCLE* deteriorated late in its second season and continued to do so until it was cancelled partway through its fourth. *The Girl from UNCLE* was high camp from moment one and it deserved to die much sooner than it did. This was episode 17 of 29, arriving in January 1967, and it should never have got this far.

Especially through inevitable comparison with the Tura Satana episode of *The Man from UNCLE*, it's horrible from moment one. It's in colour, which is fine, but I missed the stark black and white of *The Finny Foot Affair*. It felt rushed immediately, losing the measured pace of its predecessor. What's more, Stefanie Powers, who played April Dancer, looks scary. Unlike many actresses, she aged very well and looked far better as an older woman than a young one. Her sidekick, Noel Harrison, the son of Rex Harrison, is even worse; he's a caricature when he's not pretending to be a joke.

We're thrown right into the action. Dr Vladimir Toulouse is the world's foremost expert on nutrition and he's the villain of the piece to boot. He abhors violence, apparently, but still roids up an old man on a special formula, Vitamin Q, thus giving him strength enough to walk through the walls, employees and steel gates of UNCLE's headquarters as if they were made of cloth.

Because he's been threatening UNCLE, Dancer is conveniently there to watch her boss, Alexander Waverly, use a small dose of Vitamin Q to turn a live rat into a dead metal one, so she saves the day with her spray of ever useful UNCLE knockout gas. It's a pretty good start for her, but if I'm not very much mistaken, it's the last moment of substance she has until the end of the episode. If you didn't have foreknowledge that she was the star of the show, you'd think she was the comic relief, the annoying victim, the damsel in distress. But no, she's here to locate Toulouse and Vitamin Q before he extorts five million bucks out of them.

Noel Harrison plays Mark Slate, whose retarded Beatle routine is fortunately overshadowed soon enough by the character he goes to see. She's the exotic and outrageous Nadia Marcolescu, played by the glamorous Yvonne de Carlo, whose run as Lily Munster in *The*

Munsters had ended a year earlier. The rather far sighted Nadia is affectionate to say the very least, wrapping her lips around Slate as she answers the door and never letting up. She pours serious drinks too, deep dish martinis; I've seen smaller goldfish bowls! She even has a pet tiger called Percy to enforce her presence. In fact, she is exactly the sort of character who would have a mad midget lover played by a comedian.

In fact Shelley Berman goes all out as Dr Toulouse, a good deal shorter than he is because he walked on his knees in Lon Chaney style. Starting out like a monotone Peter Lorre, he soon turns into Vincent Price, presumably deliberately to match his character's arty name and that of the episode title.

It's at this point that we realise how useless our secret agents really are. Dancer climbs down the outside wall, leather clad like a reject from a Marlon Brando gang and literally falls into the room about as clumsily as possible. The punchline is that it isn't a trap, honest. She's just that clumsy and Slate is transparent enough that they're both caught without much effort on the villain's part. She even has to take some Vitamin Q to be able to take down their guard, the huge Albert with a beard, a tiny mask and no top.

Of course, the dastardly villains leave them in Albert's hands and dash off to the exotic Caribbean island of Moulin because this is Cliché City where no cliché is left unwielded. I was all ready to give up at this point, with every bumbling ineptitude on the part of the heroes merely adding to the bumbling ineptitude on the part of the writers and director of this dreck, but I had to persevere to bring you a fair review. I could put a fair case that you now owe me.

At least there's some fun to be had within the last two acts that only Yvonne de Carlo could hint at in the first half. Vladimir and Nadia are a riot of a couple, so outrageous that they'd still have been colourful in black and white. He's emphatically in charge, power apparently compensating for his lack of physical stature, but she ignores that for the most part. She flounces around back home but turns tough in Moulin: she laughs at the misfortune of others, struts around with a riding crop and calls for the deaths of her enemies.

Their back and forth is actually quite enjoyable, even though it has as much grounding in reality as the live action pinball game, which is surely the best bit of the episode even though it's an inept cheesefest. Toulouse likes playing pinball, but with the heads of his enemies as the bumpers and a battalion of toy robots as the balls, walking bombs one and all. The only reason it's the best bit is that we want him to succeed and blow up the heroes.

More enjoyable generally are the performances of Ellen Corby and Tura Satana.

Corby was at an odd point in her career, in her mid fifties but apparently good enough to believably play an older character who was uncharacteristically full of youthful vigour, courtesy of Dr Toulouse's genius in nutrition, enough to almost be the action lead of the episode. She had a substantial career on film behind her, with almost a hundred rôles as far back as Laurel and Hardy pictures in the early thirties; she debuted on a Ginger Rogers film called *Rafter Romance* in 1933. However while she earned a nomination for a supporting Oscar for 1948's *I Remember Mama*, it was a rare occasion when she got anything of substance to do. On television, she was even busier, staying that way from 1950 onwards, but she wouldn't find a rôle to make her famous until 1971 as a spritely sixty year old. From that point on, everyone knew her as Grandma Walton and she wouldn't play much else until she died in 1999.

And then there's Tura Satana as the unfortunately named Rabbit. It's perfect casting to have her play the leader of Dr Toulouse's all-female elite guard. After all, who would you rather see run an Amazon army? She looks all business when she arrives on screen at the very end of act two, the nearest to the camera of a bevy of beauties standing to attention and consuming their Vitamin Q booster tablets in a Mexican wave.

Unfortunately, writers Jay Simms and Fred Eggars, who wrote the screenplay from Simms's story, didn't seem to understand what the casting department obviously knew, so every time she's on screen is a wasted opportunity. She does well with the little she's given, and she looks great with a huge gun towards the end of the episode, but it should have been so much more. On paper, this could look like a precursor to *The Doll Squad*, but in practice it can't even come close, especially given what happens to them at the end.

By that point, I couldn't help wondering how many opportunities were wasted. On paper, this episode sounds like a blast: a midget villain creating geriatric supermen, a drunken and half blind glamour icon to back him up, a live action pinball table with bomb equipped robots and a hopped up squad of statuesque Amazonian bodyguards. How could this go wrong? Well, you only have to watch to be able to count the ways.

It isn't merely the tone, which utterly fails to tap into the camp and imbecilic charm that *Batman* carried so well, only serving to shred the style that the earliest episodes of *The Man from UNCLE* had in swathes. Perhaps it's mostly through the inability of almost every one of the characters, whether good guys or bad guys, to do anything right. Most of them are incompetent, not just the cartoon villains but also the heroes who have to carry the show and, quite obviously, the writers and producers who were behind something as incoherent as this as well.

In my view, the entire show would have been better with a tough female lead, you know, like Tura Satana. I'd watch a spy show with her as the lead any day of the week and in many ways, maybe I did. I hadn't seen Anne Francis's early female private eye show, *Honey West*, but I had seen the actress Aaron Spelling had wanted for that rôle: Honor Blackman, who had played Cathy Gale on *The Avengers* and Pussy Galore in the Bond movie *Goldfinger*. However, it was her replacement on *The Avengers* in 1965, Diana Rigg, who seems to me the closest to what Tura could have done on television.

Rigg's character, Emma Peel, was tough, smart, beautiful and occasionally outfitted in fetishistic attire. She was quintessentially English but with an exotic air to her and I don't think I'm reaching to imagine Tura Satana as a wilder American equivalent. But hey, that's hindsight. In 1967, Tura was ending her few forays into TV on a disappointing note. The missed opportunities weren't her fault.

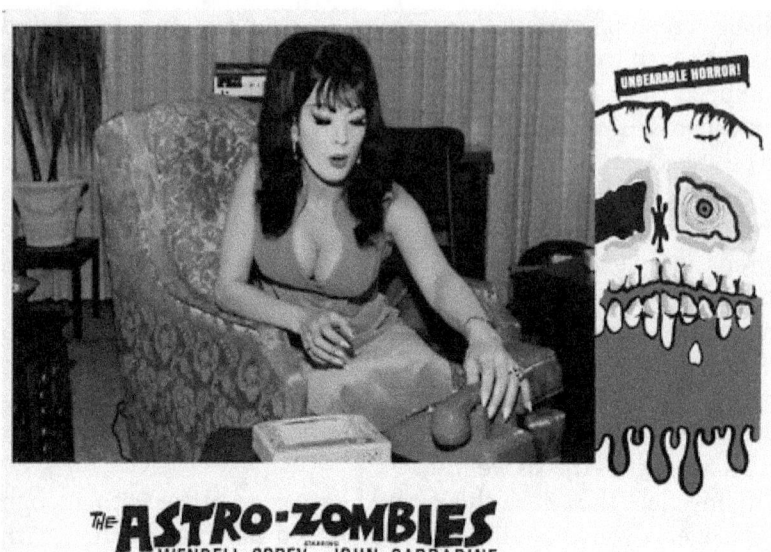

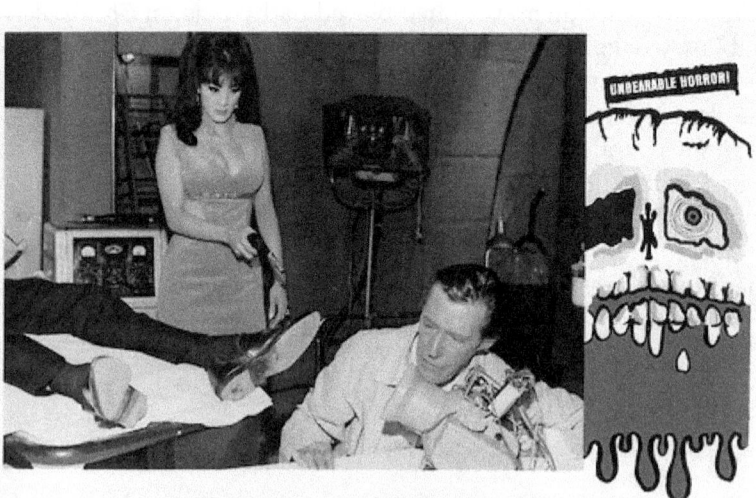

The Astro-Zombies
(1968)

Director: Ted V Mikels
Writers: Ted V Mikels and Wayne Rogers
Stars: Wendell Corey and John Carradine

Ted V Mikels is one of those names that every explorer into the worlds of exploitation film eventually discovers. He may not be one of the most talented filmmakers out there, but he's certainly one of the most colourful and, in his way, one of the most imaginative too.

Partly that's because he's done almost everything there is to be done on a film, often for his own independent movies. Mostly, though, it's because he's so impressively eclectic, not even attempting a sequel until almost forty years into his career. *The Astro-Zombies* now has three of them, which fact would surely shock anyone who saw it on original release in 1968, but back then it was something new again. His sixth film as a director, it followed a thriller (*Strike Me Deadly*), a nudie cutie (*Dr Sex*), an sexploitation movie (*One Shocking Moment* aka *Suburban Affair*), a race movie (*The Black Klansman*) and a go-go dancing flick (*Girl in Gold Boots*). At that point, horror and sci-fi were fresh territory and he had $37,000 in capital from Wayne Rogers (Trapper John from *M*A*S*H*) and his partner, Eddie Altos, to work with.

For a while we have no idea what Mikels is going for here, because it takes so long to get there. A woman with an impressive cleavage drives home to listen to crickets in her garage and apparently stand still until the man in the cool Halloween mask in the shadows finally decides to kill her with a trowel. I love the blood spatter on her white Mustang and I love the mask, but this plays about as well as the battle sequence between toy robots and tanks that accompanies the opening credits. When they're over, we watch a driver die in a crashed car, only for a sleazy weirdo to sidle up and steal his corpse. Hang on, wasn't *The Corpse Grinders* Mikels's next picture? Then a man rewinds a reel to reel tape while being driven somewhere in LA in complete silence, while a secret agent recruits a former suspect to help investigate some mutilation murders, having been cleared by the doctor who's been working undercover in his lab for the last couple of months.

These are all long and rambling scenes with lax editing and they don't appear to have anything in common, so we can't help but wonder what this story is all about. We focus on the last angle first, not least because it's the only one with dialogue. The secret agent is Holman, the undercover man is Dr Porter and the suspect is Dr Petrovich, but this is all about his research partner, Dr DeMarco, who was dismissed from the Aerospace Research Center despite widespread successes.

DeMarco is something of a genius. He had built a mechanical heart, pioneered thought wave transmission and developed a silicon skin that can withstand being hit by micro-meteorites. It was all for the space program, which is building quasi-men to hurl into orbit and talk to via computer. No, I'm not sure what led Mikels in this direction either, or what it has to do with mutilation murders, but it's obviously important and warrants the attentions of Chuck Edwards, from the Subversives division. That sounds important, right?

Before we find out where this is going, we catch up with some of those other silent subplots. The man with the reel to reel tape is taking it to Satana, a foreign agent unsurprisingly played by Tura Satana, who's exquisitely exotic in such a black and white way that she looks like a kabuki actor. Obviously cast because of her work in *Faster, Pussycat! Kill! Kill!*, she's just as tough here but she has minions to do her work for her now. She's even taught them karate moves and how to use cars as weapons, but she still has to step in and get things done. The hunching weirdo is Franchot, who works for Dr DeMarco in a sparsely furnished underground lab, obviously in a cellar. They're going to remove the dead driver's mind and put it on some sort of crystal using machinery that emits enough beeps and chirps to fill an entire Krautrock album. The missing piece of the puzzle is that the tape now with Satana comprises a lecture Dr DeMarco delivered. She wants his knowledge.

Sounds great, huh? Well, the biggest problem thus far is that it's boring. It's not incapably shot, with some decent angles and fair choreography. The sound is decent, both in what we hear and how we hear it. The story is patently ludicrous but it's fine for a B movie, as long as it ties all the strands together in the end. The acting isn't even terrible, though I wouldn't praise it too highly either and it's the supporting characters who are the most interesting.

The catch is that every shot runs on for far too long, as if there's sixty minutes of story stretched out to fill ninety so the editing is deliberately half hearted to compensate. For instance, when Franchot replaces the blood in the driver's corpse, it runs on so long that we wonder how many pints this man has. Dr DeMarco spouts so much techno-gibberish while lecturing to Franchot that we start laying bets on whether he'll ever get a line that means anything. I found these scenes play better audibly as an ambient slice of weirdness than visually.

Even at this point there's plenty of B movie potential. Tura Satana looks great in a variety of exotic costumes and she gets to pose stylishly while viciously killing CIA agents. The only thing that lets her down is the continuity: she asks questions after she's given the answers and her outfit changes colour without notice. Certainly she's a lot more interesting and efficient than her assistants, Juan and Tyros, who alternate between talented promise and imbecilic disappointment. There's mystery to Franchot too, Dr DeMarco's assistant, even though we're not convinced he even understands the English language. Certainly he never speaks and he turns and squints so often that I wanted to rewind the film and count the reused shots. He constantly appears to be on the verge of doing something outrageous, not least because he has a cute Asian girl in a bikini strapped to a table in Dr DeMarco's cellar laboratory that his master keeps distracting him away from.

Strangely, it's the leads who disappoint most. Wendell Corey is top billed as Holman, but he slurs his way through his lines as if he's had too many to drink. Maybe he had, as his career nosedived due to alcohol abuse from films like *Rear Window* and *Sorry, Wrong Number*, not to mention a stint as president of the Academy, to films like this and he died soon after its release. John Carradine is surprisingly restrained as Dr DeMarco, given the material. He played so many mad scientists that he could play them in his sleep. Maybe he finally did, or maybe I've seen enough of them that yet another one failed to register. Pseudoscience works better in small doses and this one is dished up in overdose quantities. To my mind, neither of them are worth watching, but Chuck Edwards is even worse. "You can't be all things to all people," says Dr Porter, but he hadn't been anything to anyone, except a laugh at Satana's club when he successfully completed a drinking trick.

Perhaps it's that Mikels is much better at writing female characters than male ones. Certainly the CIA agents share a lot of screen time but don't ever seem to do anything of substance. Edwards isn't the only waste of space. Holman talks a lot but never leaves his office. Dr Porter serves only as a link between other characters. Dr Petrovich is supposedly important but he never does much. Dr DeMarco, the driver for much of this story, just tinkers around in pseudo-scientific fashion but only ever interacts with Franchot. Yet the female characters are all worth watching, even if they're only in the picture to be victims. To me, the most watchable characters were Satana and Janine Norwalk, in the form of Joan Patrick, a strong redhaired lady who's like a sixties version of Shirley Manson. She's Dr Petrovich's lab assistant and Dr Porter's girlfriend, as well as being the former assistant of Dr DeMarco. She gets to act as bait too to catch the mutilation murderer.

And of course, that's the character of the title, which is plural only to suggest what Mikels couldn't deliver. He's the quasi-man, the astro-man, the astro-zombie, whatever you want to call him, and he's bizarrely enjoyable whenever we actually get to see him, which isn't often enough to my way of thinking. In keeping with the rest of the effects in the film, which range from bad to really awful, his costume consists of one Halloween mask, which is admittedly cool enough that I'd be happy to buy one. It's also fundamentally important, given that he's a mechanical monster built out of human parts (remember those mutilation murders?) rather than an actual human being. So, given that he's powered by light and unwisely chooses to attack in the dark, he needs batteries to keep him going. This prompts the logically sound but frankly hilarious concept that he has to run home with a flashlight pointed at his skull when those batteries get knocked off in a fight.

I was expecting this to be a lot worse. It's not good, make no mistake about that, but there is a story here that really does make reasonable sense. It's stupid, sure, but it's consistently stupid, at least until the glaring plot conveniences and day/night discrepancies towards the end.

Its key value is really as the beginning of the collaboration between Mikels and Satana. Given that he enjoyed powerful women enough to fill his bona fide Californian castle with a continuously rolling bevy of beauties known as 'castle women', it's hardly surprising that he was drawn to her powerful performance in *Faster, Pussycat! Kill! Kill!* For a brief time, she was one of his castle women and she's said in interviews that she enjoyed the experience. Certainly she came back for more, shooting three more films for Mikels over 37 years.

In between, Mikels made other movies, some of which he even made money on. The thirteen months he spent on this legendary trashy masterpiece didn't earn him a dime.

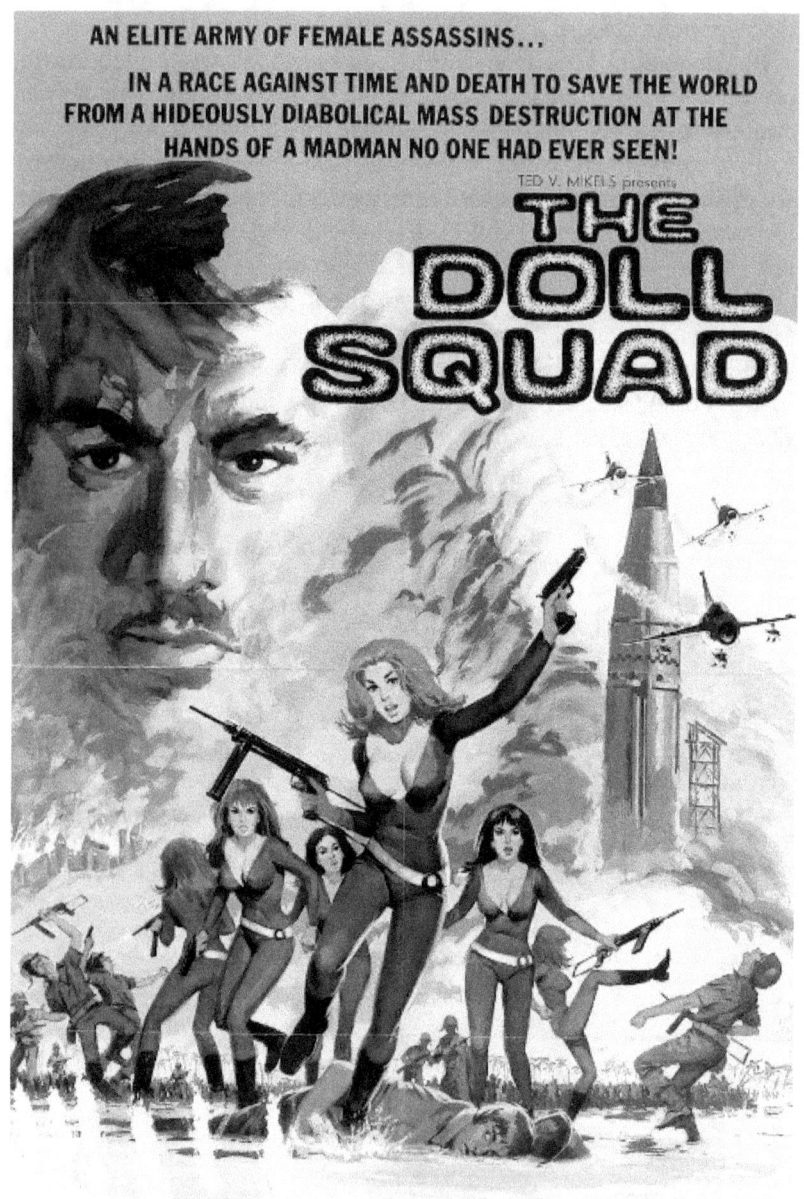

The Doll Squad
(1973)

Director: Ted V Mikels
Writers: Jack Richesin, Pam Eddy and Ted V Mikels
Stars: Michael Ansara, Francine York and Anthony Eisley

Tura Satana got to be ahead of the curve a couple of times in her career. *Our Man Flint* dealt with man-made global warming in 1966. Here, Ted V Mikels starts *The Doll Squad* with the Challenger shuttle explosion in 1973. Well, it's really the launch of a rocket called Star-Flight XII but it does seem rather prophetic, especially as it lifts off from Cape Kennedy.

The difference here is that the disintegration is deliberate, as a mysterious voice explains to Senator Stockwell, head of the Defense Committee, right after launch but before the explosion. Fortunately, he has an IBM System 360 just down the corridor, with punchcards and coloured buttons and the ability to decide from next to no information which department should attack a particular problem. This time, the teleprinter suggests the Doll Squad as the most capable to investigate, under the leadership of SO-1 Sabrina Kincaid. This is *Our Man Flint* all over again, merely with chicks kicking ass.

As you can imagine, the Doll Squad is a squad of dolls. In case you don't grasp the concept from the name or the action that unfolds in lurid negative colours behind the credits, the tagline makes things very clear. "They're beautiful!" it reads. "They're dangerous! They're deadly!" Really, that in itself is enough to warrant a viewing of *The Doll Squad*, but it proves to be pretty capable too.

Sure, it's obviously not shot with a huge budget, the quarter of a million dollars Mikels claims to have spent on it certainly not all going on the production itself. It looks a lot better than *The Corpse Grinders*, made a year earlier, and it goes back to what Mikels did best, showcasing strong women. There's a lot more consistency than in *The Astro-Zombies*: all the characters, whether male or female, seem capable and decisive, the light feels appropriate and the changes of scenery are believable. The soundtrack is dated but appropriate. It all feels like an Andy Sidaris film without boobs.

Of course, the concept is completely ludicrous. The president allows Stockwell two weeks to make an investigation before he shuts down the Star-Flight XII program, but the senator believes, on the word of a computer, that it's more than enough for Kincaid to assemble a team, all of whom have day jobs, then track down and take down the mysterious villain. Sure, whatever you say, senator. Yet, ludicrous or not, it's also exploitation genius. No wonder Tarantino borrowed the concept to unleash a Deadly Viper Assassination Squad in *Kill Bill*. It really isn't a stretch to believe that Aaron Spelling borrowed it too when he created *Charlie's Angels* three years later, especially as he was invited to the film's premiére, but Mikels was never going to win his lawsuit. While they share a lead agent named Sabrina, the Sabrina here is more like Charlie. The jeeps, boats, bikinis and flares seem consistent but instead of three angels there are eight dolls and lots of death.

Nowadays, there would be a different teaser poster released for each of the girls, not to mention their own action figure if the film succeeded, so they deserve to be introduced individually.

Most obvious by far is Francine York as Sabrina, clearly a better actor than the men who hire her. She was also more experienced, with numerous credits going back to 1961 in film and 1959 on TV. Still acting today at the age of 74, her last picture thus far is another for Mikels, *Astro Zombies: M3 - Cloned*, reprising this rôle. York had both connections and talent but sadly they somehow didn't translate to anything major on screen. Her lead rôles were in lesser genre films like *Wild Ones on Wheels* or *Space Probe Taurus*, but she could only glimpse the big time in small parts or uncredited slots in vehicles for Elvis Presley, Jerry Lewis or Marlon Brando. I should track down some of her lead rôles because she's very watchable here, for both her looks and her talent.

The girls on her team are a little more varied. The first two are quickly disposed of, so get little to do. They're Carol and Cherisse, a martial arts instructor and a scientist played by Carol Terry and Bret Zeller, though I'm not sure which is which. Judy McConnell, a former Miss Pennsylvania best known for her ten year run on *Santa Barbara*, is Elizabeth White, a librarian and psychiatrist. Tura Satana plays an exotic dancer, of course, exotically named Lavelle Sumara, but she's an expert in electronics too. She looks younger here than in *The Astro-Zombies*, though this came five years later. Leigh Christian is an Olympic swimmer called Sharon O'Connor. That leaves Jean London as a mystery girl called Kim Luval on her first doll mission, who's quickly kidnapped from an undercover gig in a carnival to be switched out with the villain's girlfriend, and Cat, played by one of Mikels's key castle women, Sherri Vernon, who also did the hair, make up and some editing.

These girls are pretty capable, for the most part, at least the ones who don't get themselves killed or kidnapped before they can do anything. They all look great, in costumes that either show a lot of skin or are tight enough to amply highlight what we can't see. They get matching jumpsuits too, with white lines to highlight their delightful profiles from the side, proving yet again that style and subterfuge are not incompatible in the world of exploitation film. Quite a few of these girls could have joined the Angels, Sherri Vernon acquitting herself particularly well.

They do benefit from one of the most outrageous plot conveniences in film history though. They know who the villain of the piece is because it's Sabrina's old boyfriend, a former colleague gone mad called Eamon O'Reilly. She recognises his voice on the message he sent to the Senator and confirms her suspicions in the computer room twenty minutes in. How's that for a shortcut to the usual investigation plot?

Given that O'Reilly is mad, it may be understandable that he doesn't seem to grasp concepts like using a fake name or disguising his voice. He's also played by Michael Ansara, whose authoritative voice is one of his most powerful attributes and surely a key reason why Mikels hired him. He nails the rôle, looking and sounding exactly as he should, even when given inane dialogue to work with. "I never make mistakes," he intones, while outlining his secret plan to take over the world to the assassin sent to kill him. Ansara nearly makes us believe O'Reilly, but not quite. Christopher Lee couldn't have done it either; it's just that out there. Everything so far has tied to his need to obtain microfilm detailing America's ballistic missile plans, but then we discover that his maniacal plan has nothing to do with ballistic missiles in the slightest. This whole thing is constructed on utterly fake foundations that fall away the moment we ask our first question about consistency.

Mikels does well here nonetheless, delivering everything he aims for. It runs along at a reasonable pace, never dragging and with something thrown in to distract us every time it might: a death scene, a bikini scene or one of the bizarre explosions that seem to be special effects on the film itself. Much has been mentioned of the various gun battles all being shot at night, a single night at that because Mikels could only get hold of one machine gun, so he handed it round to each actor he felt should use it, all during one long twelve hour shoot. Yet all that looks fine to me, if perhaps a little dark and the explosions certainly needed work. Everything else technical looks fine, with Mikels's castle ably serving as the villain's island headquarters. You can't argue at the cost when shooting in your own home. It's edited much better than *The Astro-Zombies*, lit like *The Corpse Grinders* should have been and it all feels like a coherent, if flawed, piece of work.

The biggest flaw is with the script. Mikels often has scripts sitting around for years until he can get the funding to shoot them, but this one feels like it was written on the fly, like it was always going to be about ballistic missiles, only to be changed when Mikels couldn't figure out how to make that work. After all, if he could only get one machine gun, he wasn't likely to get hold of anything that looked remotely like a ballistic missile.

The admirable build up sadly means that the various dolls in the Doll Squad get little to do. They each get their moments in the spotlight but not much more. While Tura Satana gets to take down a few enemies, it just isn't enough and she doesn't get to use any martial arts either. All the girls would have benefitted from a hand to hand combat scene or six and there's no reason why O'Reilly couldn't have had five times the guards, even if he had to have the same actors play them over and over again. More action is never a bad thing.

Yet they do enough for this to easily be seen as a feminist film. The male authority figures here, Senator Stockwell and Sabrina's boss, Victor Connelly, are capable men, unlike their equivalents in *The Astro-Zombies*, but generally the men here are villains. There's only one girl in O'Reilly's operation and she's completely useless. Basically, the good guys here are girls and the bad guys are guys. It can't get more telling than the scene where O'Reilly explains the details of his plan to a crowded room of foreign agents, all of whom are male, while Sabrina surreptitiously listens to everything in her form fitting jumpsuit with its profile defining white line. How can this scene be read if not that the world is about to be destroyed by men but there's a good looking girl ready to save it?

It's only a shame that Mikels couldn't get a sequel in place soon after, if only to give Tura Satana something worthy to work with. As it was, she vanished from the screen for almost thirty years.

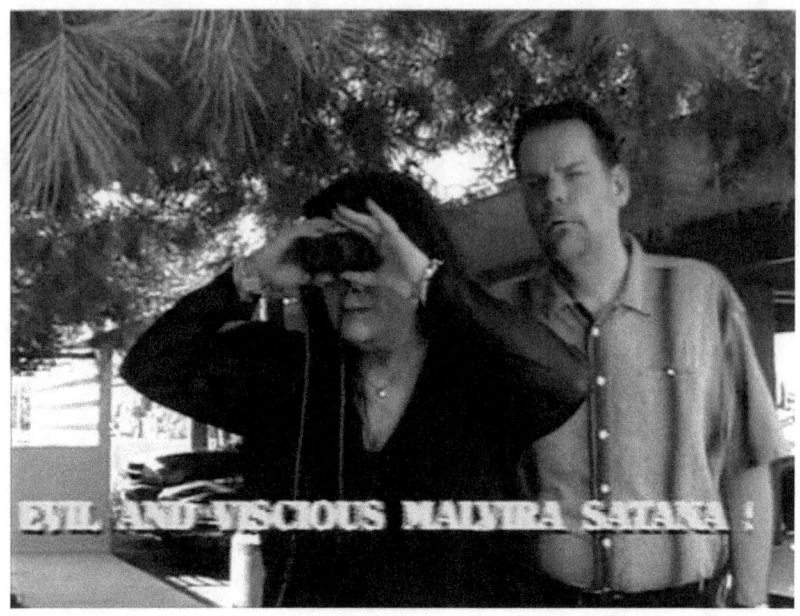

Tura's character gets a descriptive (and misspelled) text introduction!

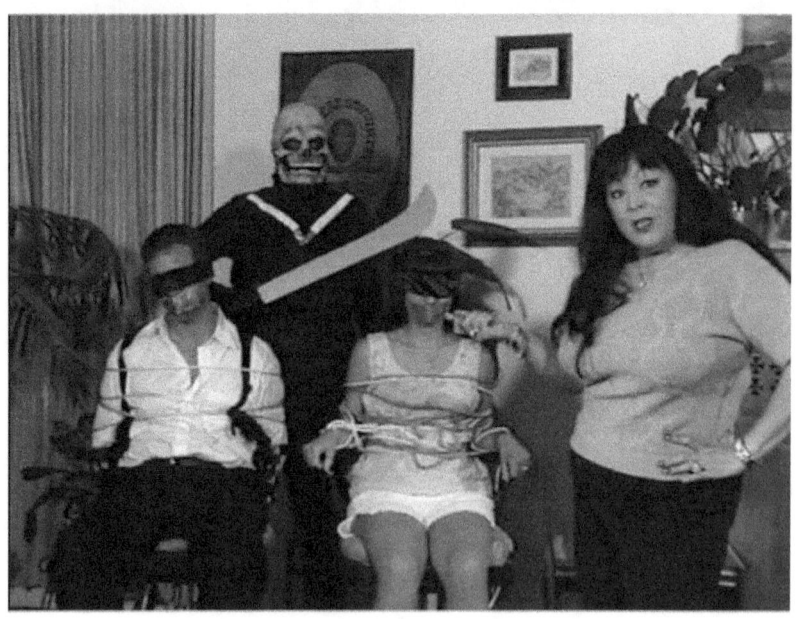

Mark of the Astro-Zombies
(2002)

Director: Ted V Mikels
Writer: Ted V Mikels
Stars: Tura Satana, Liz Renay and Brinke Stevens

The Astro-Zombies is one of those cheap B-movies that I really want to love but can't quite find the conviction to do so. It had everything it needed to succeed: an imaginative horror/scifi monster with a cool mask and a quirky gimmick, John Carradine as a mad scientist with a bizarrely hunched mute assistant and Tura Satana as a dangerous and exotic foreign agent.

Yet it fell short in almost every way. There was only a single astro-zombie for a start, even though there was nothing to the costume but the mask. He didn't get to kill often and when he did it was painfully slow. Its collection of subplots took a long while to connect together, so we were rarely sure what we should be paying attention to. Almost every scene was drawn out through lackluster editing. It looks awesome as a three minute trailer, but it didn't extend out well to feature length, ending up as little more than a lost opportunity and a sad disappointment. And a Misfits song, of course.

When filmmaker Ted V Mikels returned to the concept no less than 34 years later to shoot a sequel/reinvention, he seems to have aimed very deliberately at avoiding every single one of those complaints. In fact he begins *Mark of the Astro-Zombies* with a rampaging mob of astro-zombies, raging through a strip mall with their machetes and killing with abandon. There are literally more kills by astro-zombies within the first three minutes of this film than during its entire predecessor, and that's just the first rampage. A couple of minutes later, there's another one, with still more yet to come. The pace and editing are so fast that, for a while, we read the background as much as we hear it. Mikels doesn't even slow down to introduce characters or situations, substituting scrolling text thrown onto the screen for creative dialogue. He brings back Tura Satana for her first picture since 1973's *The Doll Squad* and even resurrects John Carradine from his eternal grave in the form of a special effect.

So you can't accuse Mikels of not paying attention to criticism, and frankly he delivers everything an astro-zombie nut might possibly request, along with a whole lot more, updating the franchise for a new generation.

Does that make this film a good one, though? Well, no. Not remotely. In many ways it's more of an unholy mess than the last one. It's a sprawling nightmare of a picture with a cast that may just include half the city of Las Vegas, most of whom couldn't act their way out of a paper bag. It's also obviously shot on video with a bizarrely inconsistent set of special effects: the CGI is primitive but actually pretty good for a 2002 movie with this lack of budget and the gore work is transparent but reasonably effective, but the aliens are awful beyond description. Most of them are like Saturday morning cartoon nightmares with half fish, half crocodile heads that don't move. Their leader, Zekith, is a humanoid reptilian, like an alien from the original V series in burned papier-maché and a barbarian robe. He's a dollar store action figure sprung to life.

And yes, aliens. In 1968, the astro-zombie was the creation of a human being, Dr DeMarco, a mad scientist sacked from the US space programme. In 2002, that hasn't changed because he's here too as a disembodied head kept alive by a rival for its insight. Tura Satana's character is the sister of the agent he killed in the first film and she seeks her revenge in this one. Yet, the astro-zombies here are created by evil aliens from a giant asteroid who, according to the opening, "have come to force their intentions upon us". Presumably "their intentions" translates into "bloody death" and little else, because their instructions to their creations are as simple as could be: "Kill! Kill! Kill!" really doesn't leave much room for misinterpretation. This is the reinvention part, this somehow being a sequel, a remake and a reboot all in one. With aliens. Who speak in the deep manipulated voices that bad cartoons use. So get used to that, OK? If you can't get past the aliens, you might as well give up right there.

As crazy as the story gets, there is one and it has a whole ensemble of characters. I got the feeling that Mikels cast anyone who agreed to show up, whenever they showed up, shot their entire parts in a single day and then spliced it all together later.

Certainly every scene with either Tura Satana or Brinke Stevens was shot over a mere two days. At least they're both experienced actors, especially Stevens, who's a delight here as Cindy Natale, a pleasingly short skirted TV reporter for News 13. It's hardly the deepest or most substantial rôle she's ever landed, but she does everything asked of her with a twinkle in her eye and a spring in her step. Except when she's kidnapped by Malvira Satana, of course. As her namesake, Tura Satana gets more to do here than she'd been given since *Faster, Pussycat! Kill! Kill!*, which was shot 37 years earlier when she was 27. She's a lot older and a lot larger here but the old Varla magic still shows when she shouts at Zokar, her obnoxious assistant.

Of course, with an alien invasion going on, if you can call a set of rampaging astro-zombies with machetes an alien invasion, the President has to be called. Here that's Ward Pennington, who in the form of the neatly named Gene Paul Jones looks rather Reagan-esque, but the similarities stop there. Pennington can't even get the Oval Office for his debriefing, because it wasn't available. What could be going on that's so important that the president can't meet in the Oval Office to remediate an alien invasion? Well, the sort that won't call in the big guns, that's who, because it's too soon. Instead he has his military attaché, Gen Kingston, assemble a crack team of doctors, scientists and experts to figure out how to respond. Yeah, that's totally what Reagan would do. Of course he wouldn't react with full military might, he'd let the general hire a "specialist in interplanetary communications" instead, who's more than a little reminiscent of George Carlin, to consult with a lecturer on remote viewing who looks like a bad fortune teller. Of course he would.

Actually, Volmar Franz, the George Carlin lookalike who plays Dr Randolph West, clearly a Lovecraft homage, is one of the few lesser names here who can actually act, even though he's only made it into one film not directed by Mikels. There are a few budding hopefuls, to be fair, but none get much screen time. Donna Hamblin is capable, but she only plays a secretary. Scott Miller lives up to his brief part as a capable FBI agent even though he tries a little too hard. He's still head and shoulders above most of the cast, who are often unintentionally hilarious. I wouldn't even call them amateur actors, as that would suggest that they actually have a calling. Most of them feel like fifty-something office workers who got stuck in scrubs or suits and given a card to read. A conspiracy theorist might suggest that Mikels hypnotised them first or drugged them with serum to make them comply with his directions, if in word only. Few of them could have heard of intonation, let alone know what it means.

Some of them are here because they're characters in real life. Second billed is Liz Renay, the sort of larger than life celebrity who makes it into John Waters movies. Hers was *Desperate Living*. Renay was a Marilyn Monroe lookalike, a stripper who worked an act with her daughter and, most notoriously, a convicted felon, earning three years as the girlfriend of mobster Mickey Cohen. She divorced five husbands and outlived two more, which helps make her rôle here as Crystal Collins, a bloated Liz Taylor-ish actress who was abducted by aliens, all the more believable. She has precisely nothing to do with the rest of the plot, being there only to add colour to proceedings. Shanti does likewise as the remote viewer, Dr Owens, with her oversize rings, clipped accent and wild make up, but she doesn't have Renay's charisma. Best known as Dr Wendy Altamura, Mikels' latter day companion, she shouldn't be on screen. "I'm very uncomfortable with what I'm getting," she says at one point and we can believe it.

There's so much in this film that it's hard to decide what to focus on next. It feels like that was a challenge for Mikels too, when trying to hold the script together. Every shot seems to bring in a new character, setting or concept, perhaps all three at once. Oh look, there's a gratuitous shower scene! Hey, is that a completely different set of three-eyed aliens? Here's Mikels in a cameo with his hair mussed up but his trademark handlebar moustache left intact. There's the disembodied head of John Carradine bickering with Tura Satana. "All you are is a bad form of taxidermy!" she tells him. "Your cerebellum has long since expired from neglect!" he replies. One minute we're at NASA, the next in a morgue and then the president's briefing suite. All of them look like hotel conference rooms with that recognisably generic decoration. And whenever we might blink, there's another horde of machete wielding astro-zombies massacring another slew of willing locals. Watching *Mark of the Astro-Zombies* feels like watching a half dozen exploitation movies thrown into a blender with scenes rearranged so that they make some vague sort of sense.

The production cost was obviously not high with Mikels shooting on digital video rather than his usual film stock, but we get past that pretty quickly. Generalising horrendously, if you make it past ten minutes, you're going to stick it out; while you're likely to shake your head at the end of it and wonder how to get that hour and a half of your life back, somewhere deep inside you're going to be a little happier for having made the effort. It does stay with you.

Never mind the aliens, there's good old fashioned fun to be had in Tura Satana's hokey auction routine, Brinke Stevens will charm everyone and I defy you not to grin a huge grin through each astro-zombie rampage. The moment it finished, I wanted to follow up with the clumsily titled *Astro-Zombies: M3 - Cloned*, with Francine York, Peaches Christ and, in her last film, Tura Satana.

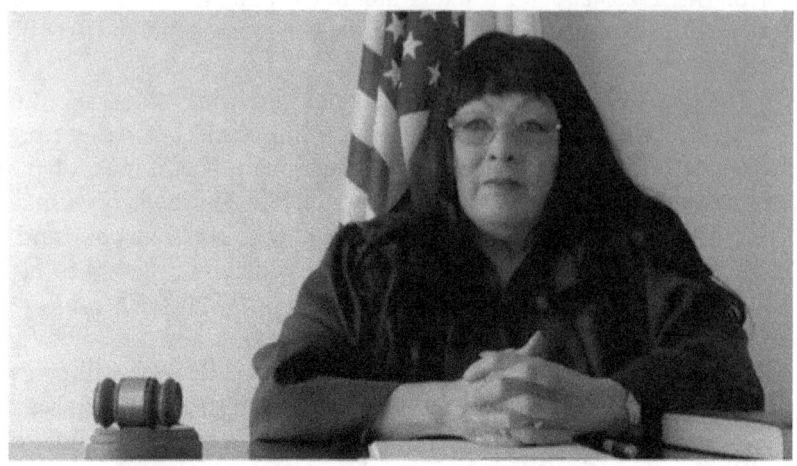

Would you want to be sentenced by Judge Tura?

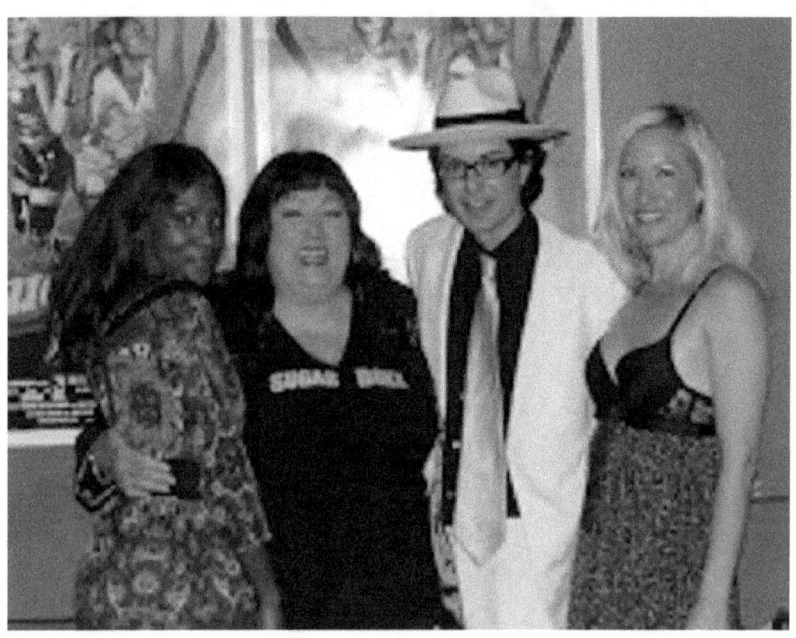

The stars and director at the Los Angeles première.

Sugar Boxx
(2009)

Director: Cody Jarrett
Writer: Cody Jarrett
Stars: Geneviere Anderson, The'la Brown, Kitten Natividad and Linda Dona

When I originally reviewed *Sugar Boxx*, a brand new, old school, women in prison flick with old school names like Kitten Natividad, Tura Satana and Jack Hill to prop up the leads, I described how good it felt to watch a genre movie made by a fan who threw onto the screen nothing but what he wanted to see as an audience member.

I still stand by that, but find it somewhat ironic to revisit it after *The Haunted World of El Superbeasto*, which I decried for exactly the same reason. To be fair, *Sugar Boxx* has a specific genre focus to which it stays true, while Rob Zombie's animated feature aimed a nod at every genre, star and gimmick that overflowed from his brain into his script. In its way, this is even truer to its source influences than the sort of grindhouse homages that Quentin Tarantino creates, for he has a habit of merging at least a couple of influences every time out and he goes full on hog wild on occasion. Here writer/director Cody Jarrett made absolutely nothing but a women in prison movie.

Most of *Sugar Boxx* unfolds within the Sugar State Women's Facility, the hardest in Florida, a women's prison run by the ruthless warden Beverly Buckner, who of course is evil, blonde and lesbian. Hundreds of women are sent her way before investigative TV journalist Val March is pointed in that direction by the aunt of one of those girls, Cheryl Jean McGossard, and she discovers a rather striking pattern to them.

Most are young, under twenty-five years old, without prior convictions and booked in Tallahassee for a combination of drug and solicitation charges. They're all sent down for hard jail time, even for first offences. And all are either innocent or at least not guilty of much except stupidity. When McGossard gives a blowjob to an undercover police officer at the beginning of the film, she has a rather ineffectual defence: "But you said you weren't a cop!" she sputters out. So off goes Cheryl Jean to Sugar State, courtesy of Judge Tura Satana, and off goes Val to find her, courtesy of Judge Jack Hill.

Val is a great character for a movie like this. She's a dedicated reporter, who researches her stories and persuades Ed, her editor, to let her try to find an undercover scoop inside Sugar State. She's cute, blonde and lesbian, naturally. And she has that one streak of mandatory blind stupidity. "What could happen in prison?" she asks Ed. "What could really happen?" she asks her girlfriend.

She clearly hasn't seen this sort of movie, which comes with its own rulebook, one that Jarrett adheres to throughout. If being sent to Sugar State by Jack Hill, the director of legendary women in prison movies, *The Big Doll House* and *The Big Bird Cage*, didn't clue her in, she really had to find out for herself. She soon gets an idea of what could happen when she speeds towards Tallahassee under the name of Angel Mullwray. She wants to be caught, which she promptly is, but I doubt she expected to be beaten by corrupt Sheriff Toll and very likely raped in the process. And she hasn't even got to Sugar State yet.

When she does get there, sashaying into the pen in her bangled top, Daisy Dukes and high heels, she's promptly deloused by Kitten Natividad, something that I'm sure a lot of folks would be happy to pay for. She also meets guards like Capt Green and Elmer Lee Fish, nasty and obnoxious folk overseeing the whipping of a girl who tried to escape, incidentally played by Tura Satana's agent, Siouxzan Perry. She quickly ends up in the office of Warden Beverly Buckner, who promptly gives her the very scoop she's been looking for on their first meeting.

There's apparently a 'special program' for inmates as cute as her, one that involves living on the ranch with a snack bar and part time light duty, in return for spending every Saturday partying on down with the very special guests of the warden. Now she merely has to gather enough evidence to prove it all, after surviving long enough to put a case together, and anyone who's seen a women in prison movie knows exactly what that's going to entail.

Actually we get a women in prison movie heavy on the topless nudity and less heavy on the blood and sadistic violence, the sinister doctor character being trimmed from an earlier version of the script. The pink underwear on show even works as a little bit of social comment, coincidentally heightened by my watching this in Maricopa County, Arizona, home of the controversial Sheriff Joe Arpaio, who didn't just pioneer putting his male prisoners in tents in pink underwear, he even offers such items for sale to the public.

Women in prison movies were never intended to win any awards for drama, but there's enough attention given to the crusading back story and enough restraint shown on the sadistic side to ensure that this could easily play well to male and female audiences and be just as worthy on future viewings, suggesting a potential cult hit. So many movies in this genre succeed only by being more sleazy than their predecessor and they rarely fare well on a second time through. This one stands up well.

Cody Jarrett must have had a silver tongue because he persuaded Geneviere Anderson to sign on as Val March, even though she didn't know women in prison movies at all before reading the script. She brings a sense of elegance to proceedings as well as some fair drama, not only getting down and sweaty with the wicked warden but also plucking heartstrings with Cheryl's Aunt Irene, ably played by the reliable Jacqueline Scott.

Scott began her genre career back in 1958 with William Castle's *Macabre*, so surely knew that women in prison movies had changed a little bit since she made *House of Women* in 1962. Anderson is probably best known for a vegetarian cooking show that she wrote, produced and hosted, called *Gen's Guiltless Gourmet*, but her most prominent rôle was as a corpse of the week on *CSI: Miami*. I could see her as a regular on a show like that. She certainly has the looks and talent for it and, while I've never seen her tilt her sunglasses, I'd rather watch her than David Caruso any day of the week.

The'la 'Rain' Brown is far more obviously acquainted with exploitation films and filmmaking and she's a sheer delight as a sassy black hooker called Loretta Sims. She ably channels a blaxploitation vibe, like a sassier Pam Grier with an animalistic Grace Jones touch and a mastery of the profane that could easily see her partner someone like Samuel L Jackson in a Tarantino movie. If we ran a drinking game around how often she uses the word 'bitch', we'd never make it through the film, but somehow it never seems out of place.

Val and Loretta end up frenemies and cohorts in the fight against the warden, something that's aided by great chemistry between the pair, which really helps to build the film. Of course, it can't hurt for them to catfight in the river in white T-shirts on their first day on work detail. That gets them a day in the hot box, which is basically just a sauna compared to what we saw in *The Bridge on the River Kwai*, at least while the sun is up. At night it's very cold indeed and they're only wearing panties.

Beyond some magic delivered by these two leading ladies, there are lots of little touches that make *Sugar Boxx* a joy to watch. Cody Jarrett, who wrote and directed, as well as performing a whole slew of the post production technical duties, obviously knows and loves his material and that shines through. There's nothing here that screams of overt self importance like so many modern takes on grindhouse genres that often hammer home their references as if we wouldn't recognise them otherwise. This is no spoof, it's a heartfelt tribute to a bygone day that I think Jarrett nails, down to the way these oppressed prisoners manage to keep their uniforms pristine, their faces made up and even highlights in their hair, without ever making a fuss about any of it. This is the sort of movie where a TV reporter knows exactly how to use a bullwhip. I loved the fact that the one good guard is a black man named Mr Tibbs but that name is never driven home with a "They call me MISTER Tibbs!" line to make it obvious.

While the story is inherently never going to hold any real surprises, Jarrett keeps it from being entirely predictable. So after the routine is run through once for appearances, Val joins the special program by giving the warden some lip service, not that much of a hardship given that she's a lesbian and Warden Beverly's voice is wonderful, part acerbic Eileen Brennan, part confident Jack Palance and part nympho porn star. Of course Val tracks down Cheryl, of course she discovers a threat to her cover and of course she gets out in the end to rumble the story, but there's more going on than that: Jarrett channels some *Switchblade Sisters* to go with *The Big Doll House* and a whole payback angle erupts. He has a lot of fun with split screens, kung fu fighting, weapons training, pimp daddies in purple outfits, the works. Yes, it's over the top but in a believably low budget way, most obviously because it really is a low budget indie picture. It can't even dream of the budget *Black Dynamite* had, for instance, but that just helps the authenticity.

It's not all good, but it's all good where it matters. Some supporting actors are wooden and none really shine but they all do what they're tasked with doing. Tura Satana and Jack Hill are spot on as judges. This may well be the best acting Satana ever did, though it's restricted to a single monologue early in the movie. The glorious Kitten Natividad obviously revelled in shouting her mouth off as Matron Mays and, while Linda Dona is no Sybil Danning as Warden Beverly, she doesn't try to be. Both could have done with more depth and more screen time, while the film deserved more blood, the machetes on the poster screaming to be put to some good use or other. Maybe some more prisoners would have helped too and some more flavour to the Sugar State pen, but that's where budget counts. It's notable how much of this film unfolds outside because Jarrett obviously didn't have budget enough to construct believable sets. The furthest he often goes is a well placed and well painted sign, but often that's all that's really needed.

Such are the breaks in pure independent cinema, films that don't merely have the word 'indie' stamped on them as a fake seal of approval by a backing studio, but which were really made outside the system by people forced to balance the freedom to shoot what they want with the inherent restrictions of the meagre resources they can muster. Modern day grindhouse filmmakers really should pay attention to this picture to learn that the unmistakable feel of passion combined with no budget is worth far more than aging effects, funky tunes and hipster dialogue. Grindhouse flicks were never about slickness and perfection. An homage like this works with soap opera dialogue and a last scene that's as stupid as it is fun, because that's the point, as much as boobs, whippings and girl on girl action.

It was clear from the screen that everything about *Sugar Boxx* was genuine and talking to Anderson, Brown and Jarrett after a local screening underlined that. If only they'd been in my front room when I watched it again at home.

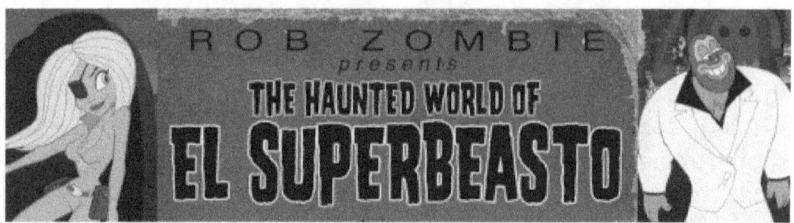

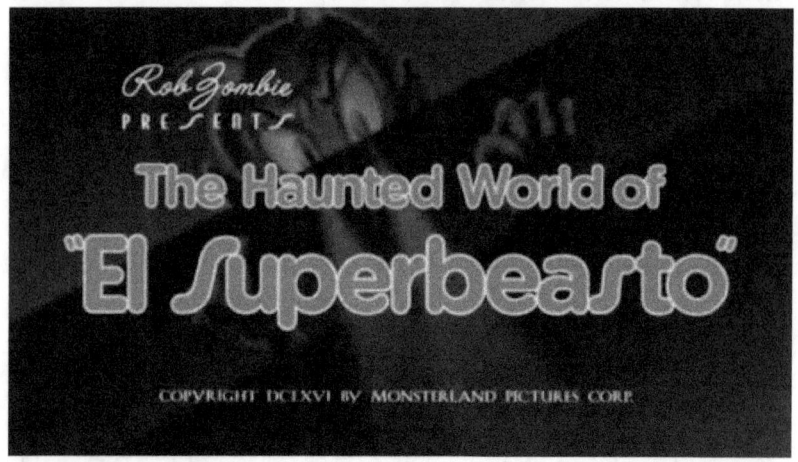

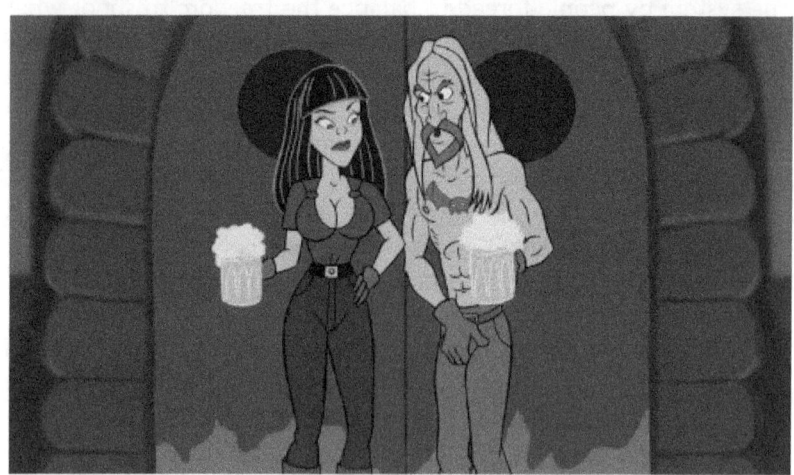

Cartoon Varla vs Cartoon Otis B Driftwood.

The Haunted World of El Superbeasto (2009)

Director: Rob Zombie
Writer: Tom Papa
Stars: Tom Papa, Sheri Moon Zombie, Rosario Dawson and Paul Giamatti

Obviously a labour of love for Rob Zombie, *The Haunted World of El Superbeasto*, an old school animated feature based on his comic book series, was stuck in production for years while other, more commercial propositions, concentrated his attention, especially the reboot of the *Halloween* franchise. However, he stuck at it and, as his name became more important within the industry, the budget ballooned from a half million dollars to ten.

The catch is that the film is so effectively an outpouring of everything that Zombie loves from a full hundred years of pop culture that the target audience is effectively him. Others may get kicks out of it, but they're only going to get a fraction of what Zombie threw in and, especially to young audiences, that fraction could end up as a tiny one indeed. I recognised a lot but I surely missed a lot too. I left it amused but unimpressed, interested more in the musical cartoon series cited as its key influence, *Sabrina and the Groovie Goolies*.

Now, *Sabrina and the Groovie Goolies* was a children's show, a spinoff of *Sabrina and the Teenage Witch*, itself a spinoff of *The Archie Comedy Hour*, all shown by CBS on network television. As you might imagine, Zombie's version isn't remotely kid friendly, though frankly it's kids who may just love it the most. It maintains a ten year old's level of humour, but transplants it into a very adult feature full of sex, violence and bad language, not to mention death. If anyone was insane enough to try to screen this on CBS, they'd need to trim it down from 77 minutes to about 10, and they'd still get complaints. Common comparisons to Ralph Bakshi's adult animations are almost entirely invalid, as the tone is utterly different. Comparisons to John Krikfalusi's *Ren & Stimpy* are fairer, as they share both a look and some of the same animators, but this film goes far beyond that show's innuendo. Zombie has said that it's what would happen "if SpongeBob and Scooby-Doo were filthy."

While it's almost impossible to focus on the big picture here because there's so much to distract us, there is an actual story and it's a pretty simple one. We're given a hero, El Superbeasto, and a villain, Dr Satan, who used to be nerdy little Steve Wachowski but turned to the diabolic side after receiving one too many wedgies at school from the hero. From his secret lair, Dr Satan searches the globe for a woman whose body sports the mark of the beast, so he can make her his unholy bride in the high school gym and so, in accordance with legend, become all-powerful, but villain and hero are destined to tussle again as Dr Satan's intended turns out to be Velvet von Black, a stripper whose magnificent mammaries El Superbeasto has fallen head over heels in lust with. To get her back and stop Dr Satan's quest for power, he needs the help of his sister, an eyepatched super agent on a quest to head off the second coming of the Third Reich. You know, the usual.

Realistically though, nobody cares about the story. We care about the characters and where they came from, because half the fun is in riding the attention deficit rollercoaster without a care in the world and the other half is in figuring out the plethora of pop culture references. El Superbeasto in particular, did nothing for me, being as egotistical as cartoonly possible and driven entirely by his appetites. That's not to detract from the voicework of Tom Papa, the stand up comedian who wrote the script from Zombie's material, because he does a great job. I just wasn't interested in the hero at all, except for the fact that he's a Mexican wrestler turned actor in a suit and a luchador mask, just like El Santo, Blue Demon and their cohorts. The movies he shoots are far more exploitational than anything I've ever seen in Mexican wrestling cinema, but it's truly refreshing for this film fan to see the lead character in an American film be a masked luchador not played by Jack Black.

I was more impressed by Suzy-X, not just because she's a bodacious and hyper version of Christina Lindberg but because she's forever kicking ass in spectacular fashion. We first meet her infiltrating a mountaintop castle full of Nazi werewolves in search of a jar that contains the disembodied but still very much alive head of Adolf Hitler. Yes, that's a reference to *They Saved Hitler's Brain*. She makes it out alive with der Führer's head, only to be chased by an army of Nazi zombies. Luckily she has her very own transforming robot sidekick, Murray, a take on the robot in the Bela Lugosi serial *The Phantom Creeps*, who is both smitten with his mistress and hornier than a ten peckered owl. Even with the innuendo stripped away for mass consumption, I'd love to see a *Suzy-X* cartoon show. Talk about action packed! Sheri Moon Zombie, who's more than a little cartoonish to begin with, is utterly perfect for the part. This is by far her best rôle and she nails it absolutely.

Of course, younger audiences aren't going to get these references and I wonder how much it will matter. Even if they haven't seen an El Santo movie they may get the Mexican wrestling concept from ¡Mucha Lucha! or *Nacho Libre*. They may not have seen *Thriller: A Cruel Picture*, but they'll recognise its influence in the Bride from Tarantino's *Kill Bill*. What they'll think of Murray, I have no idea, but it'll probably tie to anime rather than classic movie serials. I'd doubt if many even know what classic movie serials were. The whole movie is full of this sort of cultural disconnect. It even begins in black and white with an introduction, title screen and score reminiscent of the Universal version of *Frankenstein*. Most tellingly, Velvet von Black is a sure nod to old school go go dancers and blaxploitation, with Rosario Dawson's foul mouthed voicework exceeding anything I've seen from the seventies, but nowadays she's probably going to be interpreted as a Jerry Springer guest.

I can't even nail many of the references and, as a reviewer of fringe movies across the decades, I ought to do pretty well at it. While clearly there's a lot of German expressionism in Dr Satan's first appearance, I'm sure I recognise the mask he wears but I just can't place it. I swear I know where his assistant, Otto the talking gorilla with a smart screw in his head, is sourced from as well, but it eludes me for now. Of course, what felt like every B movie back in the forties had its own man in a gorilla suit, but one day I might stumble back onto the one with a screw in its head. It's difficult to concentrate on that here with so many other characters to recognise spattered up onto the screen like buckshot. The majority vanish as soon as they arrive, just there to serve as a background reference, so we have to either try to recognise what we can on the assumption that, like *Pokémon*, we can't catch 'em all, or we go back and watch the whole damn film on slow frame advance.

To illustrate the problem, let's just look at the Haunted Palace, the titty bar that El Superbeasto frequents that is itself a Roger Corman reference. He runs over Michael Myers getting there, but inside are many more characters who may or may not be deliberate references. Many certainly are: I caught Leatherface, an alien exploding from John Hurt's chest, the fifties version of *The Fly*, Jack Torrance from *The Shining*, the Bride of Frankenstein and the Christopher Lee era Count Dracula just from his first visit. Velvet von Black's routine is introduced by Peter Lorre, while Rudy Vallée croons her theme song through his megaphone. Baby and Captain Spaulding from *House of 1000 Corpses* sit at a table with Otis B Driftwood, *The Devil's Rejects* version. Later, the latter tries to get fresh with Varla from *Faster, Pussycat! Kill! Kill!* I saw Mike Wazowski from *Monsters, Inc* and the Phantom of the Opera too, but are the rest merely generic monsters in this world of Monsterland? Who did I miss?

Certainly I missed some of the guest stars. I did catch Danny Trejo as one of El Superbeasto's old homies, in a Hispanic scene that's painfully stereotypical until it's turned neatly on its head; Ken Foree as a presumed Fritz the Cat homage by the name of Luke St Luke who spends most of the picture stuck inside El Superbeasto's trousers; and Tura Satana briefly revisiting her most famous character for a mere thirteen seconds. She's denied the opportunity to take down Driftwood, which would have been fun to see but it's good to hear Varla again regardless. Bill Moseley and Sid Haig reprise their regular rôles for Zombie as Driftwood and Spaulding. Clint Howard is Joe Cthulhu, the bartender at the Haunted Palace, Cassandra Petersen is one of the vapid bimbos auditioning for El Superbeasto's kinky porn movie and Dee Wallace is... well, it turns out that she's another one of those vapid bimbos, but it took my analysing the end credits until I realised they were in order of appearance to figure that out. None of these rôles are large, but some are tiny even for cameos.

Spotting references for 77 minutes can be tiring, even under the influence, strangely a vice not brought into the story, so Zombie distracts us by making it a musical with original songs from a comedy duo called Hard & Phirm, who do a fair job of providing a versatile set of songs that don't just entertain but help provide background to some of the characters. Some descend too easily into the puerile tone and become quickly forgettable, but a few are real gems. My favourite is the recurring theme of the zombie Nazis, which is a stream of consciousness piece that describes in precise detail exactly what's going on, just like 'Weird' Al Yankovic's *Trapped in the Drive-Thru*.

It also highlights how much detail is king here, because Suzy-X's action aside, the best bits are the little bits: the Benny Hill homage, the QVC moments or El Superbeasto's *Domo Arigato, Mr Roboto* ringtone. It's a shame that they outshine the big picture, which works best when being described.

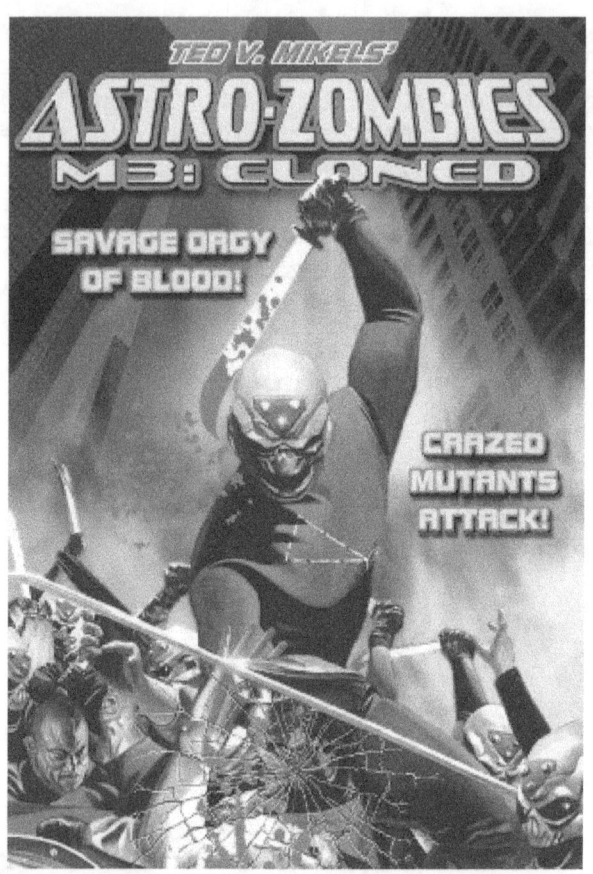

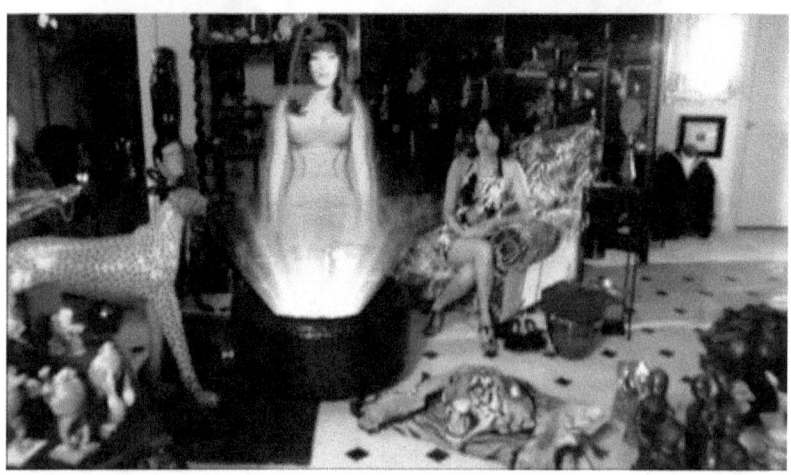

Astro-Zombies: M3 - Cloned (2010)

Director: Ted V Mikels
Writers: Ted V Mikels and Cory Udler
Stars: Fletcher Sharp and Donna Hamblin

After avoiding sequels for almost forty years, Ted V Mikels began to embrace them as the century changed. His first was *The Corpse Grinders 2* in 2000 and his second, *Mark of the Astro-Zombies* quickly followed in 2002. Then came three more originals, a couple of horror movies and a family film called *Heart of a Boy*, but Mikels apparently decided that what the world really needed most was more astro-zombies.

Initially aiming at a trilogy, to be completed by the clumsily titled *Astro-Zombies: M3 - Cloned*, Mikels has already followed it up with *Astro-Zombies: M4 - Invaders from Cyberspace*, and as he isn't remotely out of energy at 83 years young, who knows how more may yet see the light of day. Next up looks like *The Corpse Grinders 3*, but surprisingly Mikels is only serving as its executive producer, the director's chair instead being relinquished in favour of a young Spanish filmmaker, Manolito Motosierra. Perhaps he's planning to pass the torch.

As I'm a fan of the astro-zombies themselves far more than the films I've seen them in thus far, I'm not particularly against the concept of more pictures, but they haven't been working out quite like I'd hoped they would.

The first sequel fixed every one of the problems that plagued the original film, overflowing the screen with machete wielding astro-zombies rampaging through strip malls and the back streets of America. Yet it was ambitious enough in its use of early digital effects that it's painfully dated after only a decade, and the traditional effects were wildly inconsistent too. It was so full of detail that it often looked like a cinematic equivalent of the Bloomberg channel. Worst of all, the acting was, with a few notable exceptions, painfully amateurish.

Mikels solves all those issues here but returns to some of the original ones. It's almost as if he's in constant reaction mode to the last film, aiming to improve on it in every way but forgetting the lessons he learned while making it.

This means that *Astro Zombies: M3 - Cloned* isn't the next step at all, it's an amalgam of its two predecessors. In fact, it's more than that. Mikels aims a little wider than he's ever done before to combine some of his other previous work into a single chronology. There's a DC universe; well, now we have a TVM universe. So, to combat the astro-zombie menace, we're given the Doll Squad. I even noticed a couple of cans of Lotus Cat Food, tying us into *The Corpse Grinders* too.

I quite like this approach, but sadly it's done almost entirely the wrong way round. This is emphatically an astro-zombies picture with the Doll Squad only brought in at the end to clean up. I couldn't feel more strongly that the film would have been a much bigger success if these two sides had been given equal bandwidth. If this had been a Full Moon picture it would have been titled *Doll Squad vs Astro-Zombies* and that's really how the script should have been developed.

The plot is as complex and character filled as *Mark of the Astro-Zombies*, but it has a much better focus. Thankfully gone are the cheesy aliens with their papier-maché crocodile heads, the Jar Jar Binkses of the TVM universe. Gone too are characters like Crystal Collins, who was quirky and fun but entirely unrelated to the story at hand. Instead we're grounded in a traditional story that pits the US government against itself.

On one hand, we have the astro-man project, now government funded and run out of Area 51 because the military needs insane numbers of expendable killing machines. On the other hand, we have the Doll Squad, brought in to save the day, when shock horror, the astro-zombies run wild and start to massacre the general public. The subplots tie in, such as Leonard Bullock, a conspiracy theorist who writes books about this stuff, and Malvina Satana, some sort of enemy agent with her own troupe of men in black in dark sunglasses.

Many of the actors from *Mark of the Astro-Zombies* return here, but in Andy Sidaris style, none of them play the same rôles, making this something of a surreal experience. Actor Scott Blacksher described the *Astro-Zombies* sequels as "more like parallel world excursions in the Ted V Mikels' Universe."

At least the actors who shone brightest in the last film get the bigger rôles in this one. I'd called out Donna Hamblin as being worth a lot more than just a mere secretary in *Mark of the Astro-Zombies*; sure enough, this time she's playing a major character: Dr Stephanie DeMarco, the granddaughter of the creator of the astro-zombies. Volmar Franz, the George Carlin lookalike, switches from a linking character to the man in black who pressures Bullock. Scott Blacksher moves up from an angry henchman to a master sergeant with a Hitler moustache, overacting hilariously. He grew on me in the second film, playing in his words "an attack dog on a short leash," but he's like a true force of nature in the third, yakking about "cerebral cortex tampons" and hurling out lines like, "I don't want any more brain dissertations. I want vicious killing machines that I can control!"

Going further back, two ladies return from much earlier pictures. Tura Satana returns for her third astro-zombies movie and her last screen rôle, though in a rather bizarre fashion. This time she's Malvina Satana, presumably the third in a family that so carelessly manages to lose a member every time out. This sibling gets less screen time than her sisters, presumably due to health concerns, as Tura spent time in hospital around this point. Her dialogue is new, recorded specially for this film, but what we see is archive footage from *The Astro-Zombies* of her in her pink outfit, cleverly displayed as a hologram. Francine York reprises her rôle as Sabrina from *The Doll Squad*, looking great and still in charge of the squad at the age of 72, even though it's been fully 37 years since we last saw her. That's over half her lifetime, but she's going strong. Sadly, she only interacts with the story over the phone, like Henry Fonda in *Tentacles*, as she's supposedly stuck on assignment.

The thrust of the story follows the attempts of this generation's Dr DeMarco to raise a viable astro-zombie from DNA recovered from the Astro-Zombie Disintegration Grounds and then clone it. How she's supposed to achieve this, given that astro-zombies are Frankenstein-like constructs of parts from many human beings, I have no idea, but continuity has always been a tenuous concept in astro-zombie movies. This makes a lot more sense than bringing aliens into the mix like Mikels did in the last picture, though it does beggar belief that the doctor would raise her first zombie with a machete already in his hand.

I liked Donna Hamblin as Stephanie De Marco. She brags a little about feeling like God as her subject comes to life, but she's a truly dedicated scientist who won't allow herself to be distracted by things like husbands. She's also down to earth enough to wear glasses and constantly tousled hair, all the more sexy for not trying to be.

Unfortunately her superiors aren't quite so dedicated and, of course, one of them is a traitor to the cause, secretly working for the holographic Malvina Satana, who now owns the disembodied head of Dr Septimus DeMarco, Stephanie's grandfather, which chatters away in the background. Fletcher Sharp is apparently one of the focal points as Randolph, some sort of agent who fits into the chain of command somewhere, but he gets worse as the film runs on. It's only when he gets longer speeches towards the end that we realise how bad he is. Higher up the chain is Gen Ivan Mikacev, in the form of Ted V Mikels himself, who sets the project in motion at, get this, an Area 51 Bioterrorism Conference. There's just no way that could ever be misconstrued, right? He believes the US army needs man-killing machines, hundreds of thousands of the things. Mikels is good as the general, but goes way over the top as his happy hippy twin brother, Crazy Peter.

To keep us on our toes, there are a host of other characters dotted around this story who we can't fail but recognise from the previous one, even though they're in new rôles here. As Agent WQ9, Shanti takes a keen interest in the conference. She's as wonderful in her dark hat, glasses and coat as Agent WQ9 as she wasn't as Dr Owens, the remote viewer, in *Mark of the Astro-Zombies*. She works for Sen Caldwell, who had played Gen Kingston in that film. Most confusingly, the President of the United States in the last picture has been apparently demoted to just Dr DeMarco's boss here. Fortunately the army of amateur actors who woodenly read their way through cue cards as lesser characters in the last film either don't reappear in this one at all or, at least, take much smaller rôles with maybe just a single line of dialogue. Unfortunately Scott Miller doesn't return, which possibly explains why he's missing an IMDb credit for his rôle in *Mark of the Astro-Zombies.*

I mention all these characters because I get the feeling that the script grew around them. The heart of the story is simple: the army raises more astro-zombies, they go on a rampage and the Doll Squad gets called in to dispose of them. Unfortunately, getting to the rampage is a long and tedious process that seems designed mostly to give a large ensemble of actors something to do. As with the last film, I'd hazard a guess that Mikels rewrote the script every time a new actor committed to the project, entirely so that each of them would have something to do. As you can imagine, the wider picture suffers greatly from this approach, to the point that we wish everyone would quit talking and let us see some astro-zombies rampaging around somewhere with machetes. We don't get clones until 67 minutes in, very strange clones that are different shapes and sizes, but even then they escape their cloning room only to go hang out in the desert looking moody, like an emo band on a photoshoot.

It's no sooner than 79 minutes in when the action really starts. The astro-zombies go wild out in the sticks and the Doll Squad finally shows up with cool blowguns and explosive darts to take them down. It gets serious at the 85 minute mark, when their leader escapes captivity to join them. She's Queen Amazon, so named because Sara Dunn is a voluptuous bundle of curves, and she's a promising character, but she's unfortunately absent for much of the picture, having been torn away from it before she could join in by a drag queen assassin played by the legendary Peaches Christ.

It's always great to see Peaches, a midnight movie maven and champion of underground film in San Francisco, on screen again but one reading of this story could suggest that she, by neatly crippling the Doll Squad, is the reason the movie derails. Film four should have followed a movie fan back in time to assassinate the assassin and so shift the thrust of the story back to the *Doll Squad vs Astro-Zombies* concept it should always have been.

And that's how I left this film. So much is improved on *Mark of the Astro-Zombies.* The production quality is stronger, the acting is more accomplished and the effects are notably improved. Even the continuity, hardly a key focus in a Ted V Mikels picture, is more consistent. Yet on the flipside, the frenetic energy of the second film is gone too, leaving this one overlong and a little boring. It isn't like the original 1968 picture, which was boring because nothing much happened. Here, it's that what happens isn't what we want to see. We want to see a slew of rampaging astro-zombies like we were gifted with in the second film. We want to see the Doll Squad infiltrating the military and tracking down the menace at hand. *The Doll Squad* is my favourite Mikels film thus far and I was excited at the opportunity to watch them kick ass again. Unfortunately we get very little of either: leaving this scant on Doll Squad and scant on astro-zombies. So what's the point?

Velvet Glove Cast in Iron: The Films of Tura Satana

Afterword
by Cody Jarrett

The Real Pussycat

Tura Satana was so much more than an actress, legend, or cult icon. She was a force of nature. Beneath that magnificent visage was the power of an H-bomb. You could sense it, lurking right under the surface... but you weren't scared, because you knew deep down Tura was one pussycat with a heart of gold.

I loved Tura as an actor, and as a friend. On set if you told her to go through a wall, she'd go through the wall, no questions asked. If she loved you she'd do anything for you. Once she focused on something, there was no stopping her. She was determined, generous, dignified, fiercely loyal and never wavered from what she felt was right. She lived many more than nine lives, filled with the unbelievable highs and tragedies that made her what she was... larger than life.

It was amazing spending time with Tura. I really enjoyed her company. Tura was brilliantly, hilariously unpredictable. I remember the *Sugar Boxx* premiere; she was completely out of control. Right at the film's climax, she stood up in the back of the theatre and started screaming out lines of dialog just before the actors would say them onscreen. It was beyond hysterical and totally brought the house down! It was one of those moments you can't believe is actually happening. And yet the next day, there she was, quietly signing autographs by the pool and posing for photo ops. A true, classic star.

But most importantly, Tura was real. That's why people feel so connected to her, both then and now. Take her role as Varla in *Faster, Pussycat! Kill! Kill!* Varla was sexy and a total bad-ass. Now, there are lots of good looking actors who can play bad-ass, but Tura was a bad-ass. When she walked off screen and into the real world, you couldn't necessarily see the difference. I think people could feel that and it was attractive. In Varla you get the super-concentrated version; the sum total of Tura's life experience. Varla was Tura, and someone we'll never forget.

I'm thrilled to be directing Tura's documentary, which commences production in 2013. The film will be based on Tura's memoir, *The Kick-Ass Life of Tura Satana*. Siouxzan Perry (Tura's manager), myself and everyone involved are committed to making a film that, like her life, will be epic and unforgettable. Production updates can be found at http://www.turasatana.com.

She touched and influenced so many, it's high time to give her the credit she deserves.

Tura, with this we honor your memory.

Cody Jarrett
Los Angeles
April 2013

About Hal C F Astell

While he still has a day job, Hal C F Astell is a teacher by blood and a writer by inclination, which gradually morphed him into a movie reviewer. He writes primarily for Apocalypse Later, his movie review site, but also for others who ask nicely.

Born and raised in the rain of England, he's still learning about the word 'heat' after nine years in Phoenix, AZ, where he lives with his better half, Dee, in a house full of assorted critters.

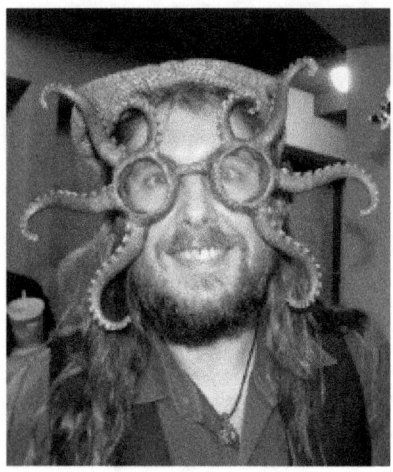

Photo by Dee Astell

Just in case you care, his favourite movie is Peter Jackson's *Bad Taste,* his favourite actor is Warren William and he thinks Carl Theodor Dreyer's *The Passion of Joan of Arc* is the best film ever made. He's always happy to talk your ears off about the joys of precodes, fifties B pictures or Asian horror movies.

He's usually easy to find at film festivals, conventions and events in Arizona because he's likely to be the only one in a kilt. He's friendly and doesn't bite unless asked.

About Apocalypse Later

Initially, Hal C F Astell wrote movie reviews for his own reference because he could never remember who the one good actor was in otherwise forgettable entries in long crime series from the forties. After a while, they became substantial enough for a dedicated blog.

As he was reviewing his way through each movie in the IMDb Top 250 list at the time for a project titled Apocalypse Later, that name promptly stuck. Originally it was just a joke with the punchline of reviewing *Apocalypse Now* last, but hey, there are worse names.

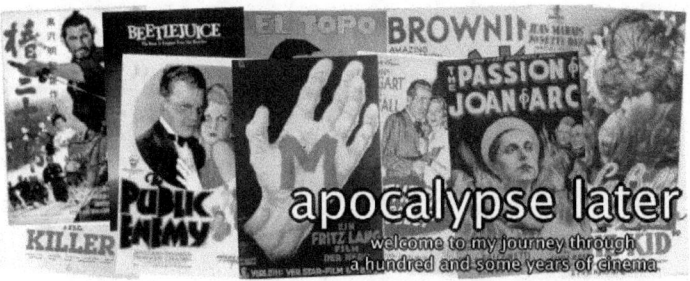

Over time, it became something of an anomaly, a movie review site full of reviews of movies most reviewers don't review. The focus is on silent films, classic films, foreign films, indie films, short films, microbudget films, obscure films, genre films, festival films... pretty much everything except modern mainstream films. It's also one of the rare sites reviewing new horror movies that doesn't kill your eyes with white text on a black background.

Think of it this way... if you want to read about *Frankenweenie*, the $39m Tim Burton animated feature from 2012, you can go to any one of ten thousand sites or even your local paper, but if you want to read about the original *Frankenweenie*, the black and white short film Burton made for Disney in 1984, you'll find that Apocalypse Later is one of the few that'll help you out. If you're interested in the unreleased movies Burton made with a bunch of colleagues at Disney who all needed to blow off steam, then there might just be somewhere other than Apocalypse Later but I wouldn't count on it. If there are any, they'll probably be good reads too.

www.ingramcontent.com/pod-product-compliance
Lightning Source LLC
Chambersburg PA
CBHW072223170526
45158CB00002BA/719